D1568045

COOKING WITH MADAME WU

YIN AND YANG RECIPES FOR HEALTH AND LONGEVITY

Cooking with Madame Wu
YIN AND YANG RECIPES FOR HEALTH AND LONGEVITY
by Madame Sylvia Wu

McGRAW-HILL BOOK COMPANY

NEW YORK   ST. LOUIS   SAN FRANCISCO   TORONTO   HAMBURG   MEXICO

1 2 3 4 5 6 7 8 9 D O C D O C 8 7 6 5 4 3

ISBN 0-07-072110-6

Library of Congress Cataloging in
Publication Data

Wu, Sylvia.
Cooking with Madame Wu.
Includes index.
1. Cookery, Chinese.
2. Macrobiotic diet—Recipes.
I. Title.

TX724.5.C5W786 1983 641.5′63 83–9868
ISBN 0–07–072110–6

Book design by Iris Weinstein.

With love and gratitude for their infinite patience and understanding, I dedicate this book to my husband, King; my sons, Patrick and George; and my daughter, Loretta, whose memory will linger with me always.

ABOUT THE AUTHOR

Sylvia Cheng Wu was born in Jiugiang, on the Yangtze River, and was brought up by her grandfather. At the outbreak of World War II, after elementary education in a convent, she moved to Shanghai and then to Hong Kong where she first met the man who is now her husband—King Yan Wu. Random chance brought her to New York where she renewed acquaintance with King. After their marriage and twelve years spent in New York City, the family, augmented by three children, moved to California.

Sylvia Wu's restaurant, "Madam Wu's Garden," was born twenty-three years ago in a small building where 50 people could sit down at one time for a fabulous meal. Her present establishment handles 300 patrons daily and plays host to such notables as Cary Grant and Stanley Marcus.

A close friend of the late Madame Sun Yat-Sen since the 1940s, Madame Wu is the author of *Memories of Madam Sun, First Lady of China*, and a cookbook, *Madame Wu's Art of Chinese Cooking*.

ACKNOWLEDGMENTS

I wish to express my deep gratitude to those who have been supportive and helpful during the last two years as work progressed on this book. I especially offer a sincere thank you to Roberta Bain, Noel Dennis, Millie Eilenberg, Joyce Hannin, Charlene Smoot, and Dr. Marcus Wong.

CONTENTS

PREFACE

The following recipes are designed to serve four people, unless otherwise indicated in individual recipes. However, in chapter 3, the banquet recipes from the Pan Hsi Restaurant and the Jing Jiang Hotel are intended for large groups.

Special Chinese ingredients used in these recipes can be purchased at Chinese groceries and markets. For a listing of these special ingredients and where to buy or order them, see chapter 6.

Chapter 7 has a helpful glossary of cooking terms for those not entirely familiar with Chinese cooking.

INTRODUCTION

It will hardly come as any great surprise to my family or friends that my life is based on traditional Chinese philosophy. From my earliest years I was taught that eating well-balanced meals containing selected herbs and spices would improve health, beauty, sexual vitality, and longevity. In order to maintain bodily balance—the Yin and the Yang—I was imbued with the ancient Chinese ritual of proper seasonal intakes of herbal soups, broths, vegetables, poultry, and other foodstuff.

While I have always followed a personal habit of selective eating—mostly fish, vegetables, and poultry—I suddenly realized that I had never actually associated it with ancient Chinese philosophy. I was just do-ing what I had been taught as a child! Yet, it is directly related to the concept of Yin and Yang as espoused by Lao-tzu, the Chinese sage of about 600 B.C. He taught there must be harmony in everything, a balance in one's life, a balance achieved out of two extremes. Yin, for example, is female, while Yang is male. Further, Yin is cold, Yang is hot; Yin is vegetable, Yang is animal; Yin descends, Yang ascends; Yin is inward, Yang is outward; Yin is heavy, Yang is light; Yin is dark and Yang is bright.

Yes, the Yin-Yang principle is present even in foods! The ingredients of each dish must complement one another, and the several dishes making up a meal should also be complementary. In this book I am endeavoring to present the art of Chinese food preparation as it relates to health and longevity, based on my heritage.

You will find included many ancient Chinese herbal recipes, special Chinese banquet recipes, many traditional and some innovative vegetarian recipes. They are from varied sources, including my own family, the famous Chinese restaurants and chefs I have visited and come to know during my extensive trips to Mainland China and throughout the world, and from friends. In that latter category I must single out my dear friend and First Lady of China, the late Madame Sun Yat-sen, whose recipes I especially cherish because she placed prime emphasis on healthy foods, faultlessly prepared and served. Too, there are recipes I invented while teaching cooking classes.

You will find some "Long Life Diet" recipes which I formulated because I have many customers in my Santa Monica restaurant who are also patients at the nearby Pritikin Longevity Center. These particular diet dishes contain no salt, sugar, or oils, allowing the natural vegetable flavors to dominate. Therefore they are low in fats, cholesterol, and refined carbohydrates.

My Long Life Diet is closely related to the traditional Chinese vegetarian diet practiced in the simple life-style of early Buddhist monks. Interestingly enough, these dishes have become generally popular with my customers, many of whom say they are not on any type of diet.

As a young girl in China I was taught that many vegetables, herbs, and spices regularly used in our cooking were considered nutritious, natural supplements to a healthy, functioning body. We always regarded the soybean, a staple in China for centuries, as being low in cholestrol and high in protein. Chinese for centuries have used a lot of onions and garlic in their cooking because they feel these are good for the heart, liver, and circulation. You will find these ingredients used in my recipes of today.

For the more adventurous cooks I have included some delightful recipes from the chefs of the renowned Pan Hsi Restaurant in Canton. During a special guest tour of the United States two years ago, these chefs demonstrated their artful techniques of preparing Chinese foods at my restaurant. One rabbit-shaped dumpling particularly captured my imagination, and so I am sharing this savory and attractive recipe with you.

In December 1982 a second team of Chinese chefs came to my restaurant. These culinary experts were from the equally famous Jing Jiang Hotel in Shanghai. For one week they prepared twenty-one-dish banquets as part of a celebration marking the twenty-second year of my restaurant. Of course, I am sharing some of their recipes with you.

This book reflects many schools of cooking, of which five are perhaps the most widely recognized, Peking (or Mandarin), Shanghai, Szechuan, Fukien, and Cantonese. When I first came to this country in the 1940s, I found that most Chinese restaurants featured Cantonese menus. Today there is much more variety. With China now open to the world, and everyone traveling about so much more, we are being introduced to a wider selection of regional dishes.

To the five major schools of Chinese cooking, I would add Hunan, which, like the Szechuan, specializes in hot, spicy foods. My particular favorite is the Honeyed Ham Hunan-Style, though the Hunan Beef with Noodles that I feature in my restaurant menu is a very popular item.

Personally, I have a great affinity for the hot and spicy dishes because I was born and grew up in Kiukiang, near the Yangtze River. Kiukiang has hot, humid summers and the mainstay of the local diet tends toward hot, spicy foods.

You will note that I have included the use of the food processor and microwave oven along with other modern methods for cooking traditional Chinese dishes. Do not worry, however, if your kitchen is not fitted with the latest technological gadgetry; you can always resort to the age-old methods of chopping with a cleaver or quick-frying! But, to simplify your Chinese cooking, it is a good idea to have some basic equipment such as a wok (14 inches in diameter), a cleaver (Dai Doh or large knife), a pair of wooden chopsticks, and a copper mesh scoop with a bamboo handle. You might also wish to purchase (and I highly recommend this) one or two earthenware pots. Be sure these pots are fitted with a tight lid so that the broth or vital juices will not evaporate during long hours of cooking.

What this book, then, is all about is a collection of authentic Chinese dishes—some old, some new, some innovative, and many that are classics, all aimed toward a good, long, and healthy life. I hope you enjoy it.

MADAME SYLVIA WU
Santa Monica, California
April 1983

1

OLD
AND
NEW
CHINESE
RECIPES

APPETIZERS

BARBECUED PORK STRIPS

1	pound pork loin
3	Tbs. dark soy sauce
3	Tbs. hoisin sauce
1	Tbs. honey
1	Tbs. red wine or sherry
2	cloves garlic, crushed
1	tsp. red wine vinegar

PREPARATION

1. Trim pork of fat and gristle, and cut with the grain into 6"-×-2" strips.

2. Combine remaining ingredients. Add pork strips, and marinate overnight in the refrigerator.

COOKING

1. Preheat oven to 400°F.

2. Remove pork from marinade and drain. Reserve marinade.

3. Place pork strips on a rack over a drip pan.

4. Barbecue for 10 minutes. Reduce heat to 300°F. Brush pork on both sides with marinade and roast for 30 minutes. Turn and brush pork on both sides again with remaining marinade. Roast for an additional 20 minutes, or less if pork is drying out too much.

5. When pork is done, remove from oven and slice into bite-size pieces. Serve immediately with dips (see SAUCES).

WU'S GARDEN RUMAKI

In Wu's Garden Restaurant we deep-fry rumaki because it is quicker and, we think, tastier. They can, however, be broiled or baked.

2	cloves garlic
2	slices gingerroot
1	scallion, cut into 4 pieces
1	Tbs. dark soy sauce
1	Tbs. red wine
2	cups water
½	pound (about 6) chicken livers
6	canned water chestnuts, halved
6	thin slices bacon, halved crosswise
1	quart vegetable oil (optional)

PREPARATION

1. Combine garlic, ginger, scallion, soy sauce, wine, and water in a saucepan and bring to a boil.

2. Add chicken livers, reduce heat, and simmer 10 minutes. Drain livers and chill before cutting.

3. Remove all gristle, veins, and fatty tissue from livers. Cut livers into 1"-×-½" pieces. Place slice of chestnut at one end of strip of bacon next to flat surface of one liver piece. Roll liver and chestnut tightly in bacon strip and secure with wooden toothpick through bacon, chestnut, and liver.

COOKING

1. To broil or bake: Preheat oven to 375°–400°F. Place rumaki on a rack over a drip pan or baking sheet. Broil or bake for 15 minutes, or until bacon is crisp.

   To deep-fry: Preheat oil in a wok or deep skillet to 400°F. Cook for 5 minutes, or until bacon is crisp.

2. Remove and drain on paper towels. Serve hot.

BARBECUED SPARERIBS

3	pounds (about 16) spareribs
3	Tbs. dark soy sauce
3	Tbs. hoisin sauce
2	Tbs. catsup
2	Tbs. honey
2	cloves garlic, finely chopped
1	Tbs. red wine (optional)

PREPARATION
1. Cut skin and fat from ribs.

2. Combine remaining ingredients, and marinate ribs overnight in refrigerator.

COOKING
1. Remove ribs from marinade, place them on a drip pan, and brush on both sides with marinade.

2. Preheat oven to 375°F. Bake ribs for 20 minutes. Reduce heat to 300°F and turn ribs over. Bake for an additional 20 minutes.

3. Remove ribs from oven to cutting board. Chop slab in half, then separate into individual ribs.

DEEP-FRIED BEEF

If one chooses not to deep-fry, the meat can be broiled in the oven on a low rack over a baking sheet to catch the drippings.

1	**pound flank steak**
2	**Tbs. dark soy sauce**
1	**tsp. light soy sauce**
1	**slice gingerroot**
2	**cloves garlic**
1	**tsp. red wine**
1	**Tbs. honey**
1	**quart vegetable oil (optional)**

PREPARATION

1. Trim steak of all fat and gristle. Use only the tender center piece.

2. Cut steak into 1-inch cubes.

3. Combine soy sauces, ginger, garlic, wine, and honey, and marinate the meat overnight in the refrigerator.

COOKING

1. Preheat a deep wok or skillet, add oil, and heat to 375°F.

2. Fry the marinated beef a few pieces at a time until done, about 2 to 3 minutes. Do not overcook.

3. Remove and drain on paper towels. Serve hot.

AVOCADO CHEESE PUFFS

When I was giving a cocktail party one night, the chef told me that we were out of crab meat. I saw a ripe avocado on the counter in the kitchen and suggested he use it instead. It was a big hit with the guests—especially Jody Jacobs. If you wish, substitute 1 cup crab meat for the avocado.

1	cup mashed ripe avocado
½	cup cream cheese
1	tsp. cornstarch
20	3-inch-square won ton wrappers
1	egg white
1	quart vegetable oil

PREPARATION

1. Mix avocado and cheese thoroughly with cornstarch until very smooth.

2. One wrapper at a time, wet each edge of the won ton skin with egg white. Put 1 teaspoon of mixture in the center of the square. Fold wrapper to form a triangle, carefully sealing the edges. Wet 2 corners of the triangle with egg white, overlap, and press firmly together. Continue until wrappers are filled.

COOKING

1. Preheat a wok or deep skillet, add oil, and heat to 375°F.

2. Deep-fry puffs for 1 minute, or until golden brown. Remove and drain on paper towels.

BUTTERFLY SHRIMP

1   pound (about 16) fresh
      shrimp

BATTER
1   cup all-purpose flour
¼   cup cornstarch
1   tsp. baking powder
½   tsp. salt
1½   cups water
1   Tbs. vegetable oil
1   egg, slightly beaten

1 quart vegetable oil

PREPARATION
1. Shell, devein, and butterfly-
   cut shrimp. Place in
   refrigerator overnight. If you
   are cooking them the same
   day, be sure to use paper
   towels to dry them
   thoroughly.

2. Combine dry ingredients for
   batter. Stir in water slowly to
   avoid lumps. Add oil and egg.
   Mix into a smooth batter. Set
   aside for 1 hour before using.

COOKING
1. Preheat a wok or deep-fryer,
   add oil, and heat to 375°F.

2. Dip each shrimp into the
   batter, allowing the excess to
   drip back into the bowl. Slip
   the shrimp slowly into the
   hot oil so that the oil does
   not splatter. Fry only 2 or 3
   shrimp at a time, turning
   after brown on one side,
   about 1 minute on each side.

3. Remove and drain on paper
   towels. Serve hot.

FRIED SHRIMP BALLS

1	pound small shrimp, shelled, cleaned, and minced
1	egg white, slightly beaten
2	tsp. cornstarch
½	tsp. salt
pinch	white pepper
1	tsp. white wine
1	tsp. vegetable oil
1	tsp. water
1	quart vegetable oil for deep-frying
½	cup toasted sesame seeds

PREPARATION

1. Place shrimp in a bowl and add egg white, cornstarch, salt, pepper, wine, oil, and water. Mix well.

2. Roll the mixture, 2 tablespoons at a time, into balls and set aside on a tray for deep-frying.

COOKING

1. Preheat a wok or deep-fryer, add oil, and heat to 375°F.

2. Drop balls carefully into hot oil. Do not crowd. Remove the balls when they rise to the surface (2 to 3 minutes) and are golden and crispy.

3. Roll shrimp balls in sesame seeds before serving.

Makes about 16 balls

VEGETARIAN SPRING ROLLS

SAUCE

1	Tbs. water
1	tsp. light soy sauce
1	tsp. cornstarch
½	tsp. sugar
2	Tbs. vegetable oil
½	cup thinly sliced black mushrooms
¼	cup thinly sliced scallions
1	cup trimmed bean sprouts
½	cup thinly sliced celery heart
½	cup thinly sliced water chestnuts
½	cup thinly sliced bamboo shoots
½	tsp. salt
24	5-inch-square won ton wrappers
1	egg, beaten
1	quart vegetable oil for deep-frying

PREPARATION

Combine water, soy sauce, cornstarch, and sugar; mix well.

COOKING

1. Preheat a wok, add 2 tablespoons vegetable oil, and heat to 350°F.

2. Add mushrooms and scallions; stir-fry for 1 to 2 minutes.

3. Add bean sprouts and celery; stir-fry for 1 minute.

4. Add water chestnuts, bamboo shoots, and salt. Stir-fry for a few seconds.

5. Remove from heat and add to soy sauce mixture. Mix well. Refrigerate several hours before wrapping for frying.

6. Brush won ton wrappers with egg. Spoon on the filling, roll very tightly, and seal the ends with egg.

7. Preheat the wok and heat oil to 350°F. Fry rolls for 2 minutes, or until brown and risen to the surface. Remove and drain on paper towels. Serve hot.

Makes 4 to 6 servings

CHICKEN SPRING ROLLS

2	Tbs. vegetable oil
1	cup chopped boiled chicken
2	cups bean sprouts
½	cup thin-sliced bamboo shoots
½	cup thin-sliced black mushrooms
½	tsp. salt
dash	white pepper
1	tsp. soy sauce
1	egg, beaten
1	package 3-inch-square won ton wrappers
1	quart vegetable oil for deep-frying

PREPARATION

1. Preheat wok to 350°F, then pour in 2 tablespoons oil, brushing bottom and sides.

2. Quick-fry chicken for a few seconds, then add the bean sprouts, bamboo shoots, mushrooms, salt, pepper, and soy sauce. Quick-fry for 2 minutes.

3. Brush egg over the wrappers. Spoon on the filling (approximately 2 tablespoons on each won ton), roll tightly, tuck in 2 sides, and seal ends with egg.

COOKING

1. Preheat a wok, add oil, and heat to 375°F.

2. Fry until rolls rise to the surface, about 2 minutes.

3. Remove and drain on paper towels. Cut each roll into 2-inch pieces and serve.

Makes 4 to 6 servings

BEEF "CHEWY"

This is my husband's specialty. In old China we didn't have chewing gum, but instead chewed on a variety of dried sweet meats, plums, and olives, which are healthier than chewing gum—no artificial colorings and sugar. Today we make large batches of beef "chewy" for the family to chew on in front of the television set.

2	pounds beef shank
¼	tsp. white pepper
3	star anise
½	tsp. five-spice powder
2	dried red chili peppers
3	slices gingerroot
¼	cup sugar
6	Tbs. dark soy sauce
2	Tbs. sherry
1	Tbs. vegetable oil

PREPARATION

1. Cut beef into roughly 3-inch chunks. Remove all fat.

2. Mix white pepper, star anise, five-spice powder, red chili pepper, and ginger.

3. Separately mix sugar, soy sauce, and sherry.

COOKING

1. Preheat a wok, add oil, and swirl it around.

2. Add beef chunks and cook over low heat for about 20 minutes (to dry out meat).

3. Add spice mixture, mix well, and cook for an additional 15 minutes. Remove the beef and cut into bite-size pieces.

4. Return the beef to the wok, and add soy sauce mixture. Cook slowly for 30 minutes.

5. Spread the beef "chewy" on a baking sheet and bake in a 200° to 225°F oven for 1 hour.

Makes 4 to 6 servings

PARCHMENT-WRAPPED CHICKEN

1   pound boned chicken
        breast

MARINADE
3   Tbs. hoisin sauce or
        catsup
1   Tbs. honey
1   Tbs. sherry
1   tsp. light soy sauce
3   slices gingerroot,
        crushed
1   scallion, finely chopped

10 to 12 5-inch squares of
        parchment paper* or
        aluminum foil
1   egg white (omit if using
        foil)
1   quart vegetable oil

        * Sheets of parchment paper are
available in Chinese grocery stores.

PREPARATION
1. Thin-slice chicken breast.

2. Combine marinade
   ingredients. Add chicken and
   marinate for 30 minutes.

3. Put 1 tablespoon marinated
   chicken in each piece of
   parchment. Fold into a
   triangular shape. Fold
   unsealed sides over ¼ inch,
   sealing with egg white.
   Repeat, then tuck in the 2
   ends left hanging below the
   base of the triangle.

COOKING
1. Preheat a wok, add oil, and
   heat to 350°F.

2. Fry 4 to 5 packets at a time,
   for 3 to 4 minutes, or until
   packets rise to the surface.

3. Remove and drain on paper
   towels. Serve packets at table,
   to be unwrapped by
   individual diners.

SHRIMP TOAST

Shrimp toast may be prepared ahead of time and stored in the freezer. Thaw and dry before deep-frying.

½   **pound shrimp, shelled, deveined, and finely chopped**
¼   **cup finely chopped water chestnuts**
¼   **tsp. light soy sauce**
¼   **tsp. sesame oil (optional)**
pinch salt
pinch pepper
4   **slices thin white bread (see Note)**
1   **quart vegetable oil**

PREPARATION

1. Combine shrimp and water chestnuts in soy sauce, sesame oil, salt, and pepper.

2. Trim bread crusts and discard. Cut each slice into 1½-inch squares.

3. Spread 1 tablespoon shrimp mixture on each piece of bread. Press firmly into bread.

COOKING

1. Preheat a wok or deep skillet, add oil, and heat to 375°F.

2. Drop shrimp bread in oil and deep-fry on both sides until they are golden brown and rise to the top of the oil.

3. Remove and drain on paper towels. Serve hot.

Note: Two-day-old bread is preferable for this recipe. If you don't have any, put fresh bread in the refrigerator overnight before using.

CHICKEN STICKS

BATTER

2   **cups all-purpose flour**
1   **cup cornstarch**
2   **tsp. baking powder**
½   **tsp. salt**
3   **cups water**
1   **egg, slightly beaten**
1½   **Tbs. vegetable oil**

8   **chicken wings**
¼   **tsp. salt**
1½   **quarts vegetable oil**
Sweet and Sour Sauce (page 171)

PREPARATION

1. Combine dry ingredients for batter in a bowl.

2. Stir in water slowly to avoid lumps. Add egg and oil. Mix into a smooth batter. Cover and refrigerate overnight. (This batter stores well and is useful to keep on hand.)

3. Separate wings into 3 pieces at the joints; discard the tips. With a sharp knife, loosen the meat from the remaining 2 sections, pulling it down to the end of the bone and over the bottom to form a ball. It will look like an umbrella that is turned inside out, or a candied apple on a stick. Salt the balls lightly.

COOKING

1. Preheat a wok or deep skillet, add oil, and heat to 375°F.

2. Dip chicken balls into batter, allowing the excess to drain off. Slip each into the hot oil and deep-fry for 7 to 10 minutes, depending upon the size of the balls.

3. Remove and drain on paper towels. Serve on platter, accompanied with Sweet and Sour Sauce as a dip.

Makes about 16 chicken sticks

SOY SAUCE EGGS

This is a delicious cocktail snack.

¼   cup dark soy sauce
1   Tbs. light soy sauce
2   Tbs. brown sugar
10   eggs, hard-boiled and
     shelled
1   tsp. sesame oil
2   sprigs Chinese parsley

COOKING
1. Combine soy sauces and
   sugar in a wok and bring to
   a gentle boil.

2. Add eggs and simmer until
   evenly coated with the
   mixture. This will take about
   10 minutes. Rotate the eggs
   so that they will stain evenly.

3. Add sesame oil and simmer
   for a few seconds.

4. Quarter eggs and serve at
   room temperature with any
   remaining cooking liquid
   over them, garnished with
   Chinese parsley.

SOUPS

湯類

HOMEMADE CHICKEN BROTH

I would like to include this recipe for chicken broth because it is an indispensable ingredient in any kitchen. Besides being the base stock for many soups, chicken broth can be used in place of water for cooking vegetables and can be added to many dishes where a bit of liquid adds to the facility of the cooking and immeasurably to the flavor. It also can be substituted in any recipe calling for monosodium glutamate. In addition, we Chinese feel it is a very healthy item in the diet. It is mild, yet tasty and quite easy to digest.

Working women (and men) may find canned chicken broth quicker and easier to use. I find no fault with that and use it in much of my own cooking. But for anyone who cannot have salt, it is best to make one's own broth. It is a simple process.

1. Place 1 stewing chicken (from which all pockets of fat have been cut away) into a pot and cover the chicken with boiling water. Add 2 slices of fresh gingerroot. Simmer for 1 to 2 hours, depending on how you want to use the chicken meat (and therefore how well cooked you want it to be). To obtain the best flavor for broth, however, the chicken should cook at least 2 hours.

2. Take the pot from the stove; remove the chicken and allow the liquid to cool before refrigerating. When completely cold, take from refrigerator and remove all fat that has congealed on top. You will now have chicken broth that is ready to use. It can be stored in the refrigerator for at least 2 weeks if it is brought to a boil every other day and returned to its container (preferably glass). If it is stored in the freezer, it will keep for several weeks.

Note: The cooked, boned chicken can be used for the Shredded Chicken Salad recipe in this book, or any other recipe calling for cooked chicken meat.

19

PEASANT CHICKEN GIBLETS AND FUZZY MELON SOUP

giblets (hearts, livers, and
      gizzards) from 2
      chickens
2   slices gingerroot
2   cups chicken broth
2   cups water
1   fuzzy melon (about 1
      pound)
1   Tbs. sherry
1   scallion, chopped
few drops sesame oil (optional)
white pepper to taste

PREPARATION
1. Wash giblets; drain. Cut giblets into thin slices, eliminating the tough outer skins and gristle.

2. Wash and peel melon. Cut in half lengthwise, then cut into ¼-inch slices.

COOKING
1. In a pot, combine giblets with ginger, chicken broth, and water. Bring giblets to a boil and boil gently for 20 minutes.

2. Add melon and boil gently for 10 minutes.

3. Add sherry, scallion, sesame oil, and pepper. Stir well. Serve hot.

PIGS' FEET AND PEANUT SOUP

3	pigs' feet
1	slice gingerroot
½	cup shelled raw peanuts
3	cups chicken broth
2	cups water
1	scallion, chopped
dash white pepper	

PREPARATION

1. Put pigs' feet into a pot with ginger and enough water to cover. Bring to a boil and boil gently for 5 minutes.

2. Discard water and ginger. Rinse pigs' feet, then chop into 2-inch pieces.

3. Soak peanuts in hot water for 15 to 20 minutes. Remove skins.

COOKING

1. Bring pigs' feet, chicken broth, water, and peanuts to a boil. Cover and boil gently for 2 hours, or until the pigs' feet are very tender.

2. Add scallion and pepper. Serve hot.

BIRD'S NEST SOUP

This was one of Madame Sun Yat-sen's favorite recipes.

4	ounces dry bird's nest
1	quart water
3	cups chicken broth
¼	cup minced chicken breast
¼	cup minced Virginia ham
1	egg white
½	tsp. salt

PREPARATION

1. Cover bird's nest with cold water and soak overnight.

2. Drain and carefully remove any foreign material from nest. Place cleaned bird's nest into 1 quart boiling water. Boil for 30 minutes.

3. Drain and rinse nest with cold water.

COOKING

1. Place nest into a pot of chicken broth and water. Bring to a boil over low heat. Boil for 1 hour.

2. Add chicken and boil for 5 minutes.

3. Add ham. Beat egg white into soup. Add salt. Serve hot.

Makes 4 to 6 servings

SHARK'S FIN SOUP

The Head of State of Malaysia came into my restaurant one evening for dinner and he ordered Shark's Fin Soup. When I spoke to him, he told me he was recovering from an operation and had ordered the soup because of its legendary health benefits.

Orientals consider shark's fin soup to be full of the "right kinds of vitamins for men," and if a person is very rich, he or she eats the soup daily to engender good health.

Shark's fin soup is always served at important banquets, and the price of a banquet can be easily guessed by the quantity of shark's fins served! Guests are really impressed when a whole platter of large fins is served.

4	ounces dried shark's fin
1	slice gingerroot (about ½ inch)
3	cups chicken broth
3	cups water
½	cup minced chicken breast
¼	cup minced Virginia ham
2	tsp. cornstarch blended into 2 Tbs. water
¾	tsp. salt
1	tsp. light soy sauce
1	tsp. red wine or sherry
2	egg yolks, mashed (optional, see Note)

PREPARATION

1. Cover shark's fin with cold water and soak overnight.

2. Add ginger and boil over medium heat for 3 hours. Drain and discard ginger.

COOKING

1. Place drained shark's fin into a soup pot. Add chicken broth and water. Boil over low heat for 2 hours.

2. Add chicken and ham. Boil for 10 minutes.

3. Add cornstarch mixture and boil for 2 minutes. Add salt, soy sauce, wine, and egg yolks. Stir in and serve.

Makes 4 to 6 servings

SALT FISH BEAN CURD SOUP

This is an old China recipe.

1	small piece (2″×2″) salt fish
2	slices gingerroot
2	squares bean curd
2	cups chicken broth
2	cups water
⅛	tsp. white pepper
1	scallion, chopped

PREPARATION

1. Rinse salt fish and cut into 6 to 8 small pieces.

2. Cut ginger into thin strips.

3. Cut each bean curd into 8 to 10 pieces.

COOKING

1. In a large pot combine salt fish, ginger, chicken broth, and water. Bring to a boil.

2. Add bean curd and white pepper. Lower heat and simmer for 1 hour.

3. Turn off heat and add scallion. Serve hot.

WINTER MELON SOUP

1   **winter melon (approximately 1 foot in length)**
3   **cups chicken broth**
3   **cups water**
1   **cup diced uncooked chicken breast**
¼   **cup diced Virginia ham**
¼   **cup canned lotus seeds**
¼   **cup diced canned bamboo shoots**
¼   **cup diced canned abalone**

PREPARATION

1. Wash melon and slice off the top about 3 inches from the stem. Scoop out the pulp and seeds.

2. Make "tiger teeth" notches about ¾ inches deep around the rim of the melon. Remove outer skin from the teeth. Dice fleshy part of removed notches to use in soup.

3. Place melon in a heatproof bowl and set aside.

COOKING

1. Put chicken broth, water, chicken, ham, lotus seeds, bamboo shoots, and diced melon pieces in a soup kettle; simmer for 1 hour.

2. Put soup in scooped-out melon.

3. Into the bottom of a deep kettle, pour about 3 inches boiling water. Using a rack with lifting handles, place the bowl with the melon onto the rack and lower into the kettle. Cover and steam over medium heat for 2 hours. Add additional boiling water to keep water level in kettle at 3 inches. Melon will be done when its flesh is translucent.

4. Just before lifting out melon, add abalone to soup and steam for 1 minute (do not overcook).

5. Gently scoop some of the tender melon from the inside with each serving. Do not scoop from bottom or too deeply from sides, or the soup will run out.

Makes 6 to 8 servings

HOT AND SOUR FISH SOUP

¼	pound sole, sea bass, or red snapper fillets
2	slices gingerroot, cut into thin strips
1	tsp. sherry
3	cups chicken broth
1	cup water
2	Tbs. vinegar (red wine vinegar, or Chekiang vinegar, if available)
¼	tsp. hot chili oil or hot chili sauce
2	tsp. cornstarch dissolved in 3 Tbs. water
1	scallion, chopped
2	sprigs Chinese parsley
1	egg, slightly beaten

PREPARATION
1. Cut fish into thin slices.

2. Mix fish with ginger and sherry, and set aside.

COOKING
1. Bring chicken broth and water to a boil. Add vinegar and chili oil. Thicken with cornstarch mixture and return to a boil.

2. Add marinated fish. Turn heat to low. Add scallion and parsley. Simmer for 3 minutes.

3. Turn off heat, but do not remove pot from burner. Slowly stir in egg. Serve hot.

WATERCRESS SOUP

This recipe, adapted for the Long Life Diet, is a simplified version of an old peasant-style Chinese soup. In the old days, pork bones were used instead of chicken broth, and they were simmered for hours in water with a bunch of watercress, stems and all. The resulting broth was drunk as a cleansing agent for the system.

3   **cups chicken broth**
2   **cups water**
1   **bunch watercress, leaves only**

COOKING

1. In a soup pot, bring chicken broth and water to a boil over high heat.

2. Add watercress. Cover and return to a boil. (Keep the pot covered while cooking or the watercress will turn yellow.) Serve as soon as the boil is reached.

MUSHROOM SPINACH SOUP

¼	pound spinach
2	cups chicken broth
2	cups water
1	tsp. salt
¼	cup minced lean pork
4	ounces canned white mushrooms, halved

PREPARATION

1. Cut stems off spinach. Soak spinach in cold water; wash and rinse thoroughly.

2. Drain spinach and cut into 2-inch lengths.

COOKING

1. In a pot, bring chicken broth and water to a boil. Add salt.

2. Add pork and boil for 15 minutes.

3. Add spinach and mushrooms. Bring to a boil. Then simmer for about 5 minutes. Serve hot.

CABBAGE AND TOMATO SOUP

Part of the Long Life Diet, this recipe appears by popular demand.

3	cups chicken broth
1	cup water
1	cup sliced Chinese white cabbage or regular cabbage
1	cup chopped tomato
1	tsp. chopped gingerroot
2	Tbs. chopped scallion
¼	tsp. white pepper

COOKING

1. In a pot, bring chicken broth and water to a rolling boil. Add cabbage. Cook for 2 to 3 minutes.

2. Add tomato and cook for 2 minutes.

3. Add ginger and stir for a few seconds.

4. Turn off heat. Add scallion and pepper and stir well. Serve hot.

LOTUS ROOT, DRAGON SEED, AND LEAN PORK SOUP

This recipe reminds me of when I was a little girl living with my grandfather. One of our tenants was expecting a baby. Her midwife gave her dragon-seed tea to hasten the birth, and the moment she drank it the baby was born. Chinese believe in dragon-seed meat as a healthy remedy. This soup was one of Madame Sun's favorites.

2	ounces dried dragon-seed meat
½	pound lean pork
4	cups water
1	pound lotus root
salt to taste	

PREPARATION

1. Soak dragon-seed meat in cold water for 10 minutes.

2. Cut pork into 2 pieces and add to the 4 cups water in a pot.

3. Peel lotus root and cut diagonally into ¼-inch slices.

COOKING

1. Add soaked dragon-seed meat to pork and water and bring to a boil. Reduce heat and boil gently for about 30 minutes.

2. Add lotus root. Boil gently for about 1 hour. Add salt to taste. Serve hot.

CHINESE RADISH AND DRIED SCALLOP SOUP

During the turmoil of the late 1930s, when I was still in Shanghai, I visited a friend of my sister who told me she was suffering from cold sores around her mouth because of a lack of pork, for she had no money. I felt so sorry for her that without hesitation, I took my gold watch off my wrist and gave it to her to pawn and buy herself some pork. Later, she wrote that she bought 10 pounds each of pork and radishes with the money she got for my watch. She made a great pot of soup and her family and friends had a feast—and the sores were no more!

6   dried scallops
1   pound lean pork
      (optional)
1   pound Chinese white
      radish or icicle
      radishes
3   cups chicken broth
3   cups water
salt and pepper to taste

PREPARATION
1. Soak dried scallops in warm water for about 30 minutes.

2. Cut pork into bite-size pieces. Place in a wok, cover with some water, and boil for 5 minutes. Discard water and set pork aside.

3. Peel and cut radishes into large rounds. Combine with chicken broth and water in a large pot.

COOKING
1. Bring radishes, chicken broth, and water to a boil.

2. Add soaked scallops and pork. Reduce heat and boil gently for 1 hour.

3. Season with salt and pepper to taste.

ABALONE AND BLACK MUSHROOM SOUP

4	large dried black mushrooms
1	8-ounce can abalone, liquid reserved
1	cup chicken broth
3	cups water

PREPARATION
1. Soak mushrooms in hot water for 15 minutes. Reserve liquid. Cut each mushroom into 3 pieces.

2. Cut abalone into thin slices.

3. In a large pot, pour in chicken broth and water. Add reserved abalone liquid.

COOKING
1. Add mushroom liquid to chicken broth mixture. Bring to a boil.

2. Add mushrooms and simmer for 20 minutes.

3. Add abalone. Bring to a boil and serve immediately. (Do not overcook abalone.)

CHICKEN ASPARAGUS SOUP

3   cups chicken broth
1¼   cups water
1   cup minced chicken
1   cup cut-up fresh or
      frozen asparagus
1   Tbs. cornstarch
      dissolved in 3 Tbs.
      water
2   egg whites, slightly
      beaten
1   scallion, diced
dash white pepper

COOKING

1. In a pot, bring chicken broth
   and water to a rolling boil.
   Reduce heat to medium-high.

2. Add chicken and asparagus;
   boil for 5 to 7 minutes.

3. Add cornstarch mixture and
   stir well.

4. Turn off heat and stir egg
   slowly into soup.

5. Add scallion and pepper.
   Serve hot.

CHICKEN BARLEY SOUP

This is a Long Life Diet recipe. Many doctors consider barley good for lowering high blood pressure.

¼	cup barley
3	cups chicken broth
3	cups water
¼	pound chicken breast, minced

PREPARATION
Wash barley. Soak in some water 10 minutes and drain.

COOKING
1. In a pot, bring barley, chicken broth, and water to a boil. Simmer for about 30 minutes, or until the barley is soft.

2. Add chicken. Stir and bring to a boil; reduce heat and simmer about 20 minutes.

CHICKEN FEET, MUSHROOM, AND DRIED SCALLOP SOUP

In China this soup is considered a delicacy and is served largely at banquets. The Chinese believe that if you eat chicken feet, it is good for your own feet.

4	dried scallops
8	large dried black mushrooms
12	chicken feet, nails cut off
1	slice gingerroot
2	14-ounce cans chicken broth
4	cups water

PREPARATION

1. Soak scallops and mushrooms in some water for 2 hours or longer.

2. Wash and drain chicken feet.

COOKING

1. In a large pot combine ingredients. Bring to a boil; boil gently for 1 hour.

2. Reduce heat and simmer for an additional 2 hours. (Add more water if needed to maintain the same volume.)

SCALDED FISH AND CHINESE PARSLEY SOUP

½   pound sole or freshwater fish fillets, cut into thin slices

1   scallion, cut into thin strips

6   slices gingerroot, cut into thin strips

½   bunch (about 1 ounce) Chinese parsley, stems removed

3   cups chicken broth

1   cup water

white pepper to taste

PREPARATION

1. Arrange fish around the inside of a soup tureen.

2. Place scallion, ginger, and Chinese parsley in the center.

COOKING

1. Bring chicken broth and water to a rolling boil.

2. Ladle boiling broth immediately onto contents of tureen. The boiling broth will scald the fish without overcooking it.

3. Season with pepper to taste and serve in individual soup bowls.

EGG DROP SOUP

3	cups chicken broth
1	cup water
2	Tbs. cornstarch dissolved in ¼ cup water
1	egg, slightly beaten
1	tsp. sesame oil
1	Tbs. chopped scallion

COOKING
1. In a large pot, bring chicken broth and water to a boil. Thicken with cornstarch mixture and return to a boil.

2. Turn off heat and slowly stir in egg.

3. Add sesame oil and scallion. Serve hot.

SOYBEAN SPROUTS AND BEAN CURD SOUP

Soybean sprouts add to the healthfulness of this Long Life Diet soup. They are available, however, only in Chinese markets. Regular bean sprouts may be substituted, but should be cooked for a shorter time.

3   cups chicken broth
1   cup water
1   cup trimmed soybean
        sprouts
¼   cup fresh or frozen green
        peas
2   squares bean curd, sliced
        into 1-inch pieces
2   egg whites, slightly
        beaten
2   Tbs. chopped scallion
white pepper to taste

COOKING

1. In a pot, bring chicken broth and water to a rolling boil.

2. Add soybean sprouts and fresh peas. (If using frozen peas, add with bean curd in step 3.) Cook for 2 minutes.

3. Add bean curd. Cook for 2 minutes.

4. Slowly drop egg whites into the soup and stir gently.

5. Add scallion and pepper. Serve hot.

BOK CHOY BEAN CURD SOUP

¼	pound bok choy
2	squares bean curd
2	cans chicken broth
1	can water
2	slices gingerroot
1	scallion, chopped (optional)

salt to taste

PREPARATION

1. Wash and clean bok choy. Cut into 1-inch pieces.

2. Cut each bean curd into 8 to 10 pieces.

COOKING

1. In a large pot, bring chicken broth, water, bok choy, and ginger to a boil.

2. Add bean curd and boil gently for 30 seconds.

3. Turn off heat and add scallion. Add salt to taste.

SEAWEED BEAN CURD SOUP

8	sheets dried seaweed
3	cups chicken broth
1	cup water
5	slices gingerroot, cut into thin strips
½	cup minced chicken breast
½	cup diced water chestnuts, canned or fresh
2	squares bean curd, diced
1	scallion, diced
1	tsp. light soy sauce

PREPARATION
Soak seaweed in some cold water for 5 minutes. Drain.

COOKING
1. In a pot, bring chicken broth, water, and ginger to a boil. Add chicken and simmer for 10 minutes.

2. Add water chestnuts and bean curd. Simmer for 5 minutes.

3. Add seaweed, scallion, and soy sauce. Simmer for 1 minute. Serve hot.

CHICKEN CREAM OF CORN SOUP

1	17-ounce can cream-style corn
1	14-ounce can chicken broth, fat skimmed off
½	can water
1	Tbs. cornstarch dissolved in 3 Tbs. water
2	eggs, slightly beaten

COOKING

1. In a pot, bring corn, chicken broth, and water to a rolling boil.

2. Add cornstarch mixture slowly and stir in thoroughly.

3. Turn off heat. Pour in eggs in a thin stream, stirring constantly. Serve hot.

CHICKEN AND MIXED GREENS SOUP

Part of the Long-Life Diet.

¼   cup dried black mushrooms
3   cups chicken broth
1   cup water
½   cup sliced chicken
½   cup thin-sliced Chinese white cabbage
¼   cup thin-sliced water chestnuts
¼   cup thin-sliced bamboo shoots
¼   cup thin-sliced Chinese pea pods
1   tsp. thin-sliced scallion
¼   tsp. thin-sliced gingerroot

PREPARATION
1. Clean mushrooms thoroughly and soak for 1 hour.

2. Drain and thin-slice.

COOKING
1. In a pot, bring chicken broth and water to a rolling boil. Add sliced chicken. Reduce heat to medium-high and cook for 3 to 5 minutes.

2. Add mushrooms, Chinese cabbage, and water chestnuts. Cook for 2 minutes.

3. Add bamboo shoots and pea pods. Cook for 1 minute.

4. Stir in scallion and ginger. Serve hot.

ENTRÉES

| Beef and Pork | 肉類 | |

WU'S BEEF WITH WATERCRESS

1   **pound filet mignon or flank steak, trimmed**

MARINADE
1   **Tbs. vegetable oil**
1   **Tbs. dark soy sauce**
1   **Tbs. hoisin sauce**
1   **tsp. red wine**
1   **Tbs. cornstarch**

THICKENING SAUCE
1   **Tbs. oyster sauce**
1   **Tbs. dark soy sauce**
1   **Tbs. water**
1   **tsp. honey**
1   **tsp. cornstarch**

1   **pound watercress**
1   **cup chicken broth**
5   **Tbs. vegetable oil**
1   **small white onion, coarsely chopped**

PREPARATION

1. Cut meat across the grain into 1"-×-2" strips.

2. Combine marinade ingredients and mix well. Marinate beef for an hour or more.

3. Combine thickening sauce ingredients.

4. Clean watercress. Discard all tough leaves and stems; use only tender parts.

COOKING

1. Bring chicken broth to a boil in a preheated wok or deep skillet. Add watercress and boil for 1 minute.

2. Discard chicken broth, drain watercress and place on a serving platter. Keep warm.

3. Preheat a wok and swirl side and bottom of wok with oil over high heat. Add onion and stir-fry for 1 minute.

4. Add marinated beef and cook for an additional 2 minutes. Stir very little or the meat will become watery.

5. Spread beef and onion to edge of wok, making a well in the center. Add thickening sauce to well. When the sauce is boiling, quickly stir in beef and onion, mixing thoroughly.

6. Remove from heat and spoon the beef mixture onto the watercress; do not mix. Serve immediately.

BEEF WITH CAULIFLOWER

1   **pound flank steak,
        trimmed**

MARINADE
1   **tsp. light soy sauce**
1   **tsp. honey**
1   **Tbs. sherry**
1   **Tbs. cornstarch**
1   **Tbs. vegetable oil**
1   **slice gingerroot**

5   **Tbs. vegetable oil**
2   **cloves garlic, minced**
2   **cups halved cauliflower
        florets**
¼   **cup chicken broth**
¼   **tsp. salt (optional)**

PREPARATION
1. Slice steak across the grain
   into thin 2-inch pieces.

2. Combine marinade
   ingredients and mix well.
   Marinate beef for 30 minutes.

COOKING
1. Preheat a wok and add 2
   tablespoons oil. When hot,
   add a clove of garlic and stir-
   fry for a few seconds, then
   discard.

2. Add cauliflower and stir-fry
   for a few seconds.

3. Add chicken broth and cook
   for 5 minutes, or until
   cauliflower is tender. Place on
   serving platter and keep
   warm.

4. Heat the remaining 3
   tablespoons oil. Add
   remaining garlic. Stir-fry for
   a few seconds and then
   discard garlic.

5. Add marinated beef and salt.
   Stir-fry for 2 to 3 minutes,
   or until the beef is just done.
   Spoon beef and juices over
   cauliflower. Serve
   immediately.

BEEF WITH ASPARAGUS IN BLACK BEAN SAUCE

1	**pound flank steak, trimmed**

MARINADE
1	**Tbs. dark soy sauce**
1	**Tbs. vegetable oil**
1	**Tbs. sherry**
1	**tsp. honey**
2	**tsp. cornstarch**

1	**clove garlic**
1	**tsp. black bean paste**
½	**pound asparagus**
5	**Tbs. vegetable oil**
¼	**cup chicken broth**

PREPARATION

1. Cut flank steak across grain into thin bite-size pieces.

2. Combine marinade ingredients and mix well. Marinate beef for 30 minutes.

3. Crush garlic and add to black bean paste. Mix well.

4. Clean asparagus and discard tough base stems. Peel the tips of the asparagus with potato peeler and slant-cut into thin slices.

COOKING

1. Preheat a wok and add 2 tablespoons oil. When hot, add black bean paste and stir-fry for a few seconds.

2. Add asparagus and stir-fry for a few seconds.

3. Add chicken broth and stir-fry for 1 minute, or until asparagus is tender. Remove asparagus and broth, if any, from wok and keep warm.

4. Heat the remaining 3 tablespoons oil. Add beef and stir-fry for 2 to 3 minutes, or until beef is just done.

5. Return asparagus to the wok. Stir-fry for 1 minute. Serve hot.

BEEF WITH GREEN PEPPER AND ONION

½   pound flank steak,
        trimmed

MARINADE
1   Tbs. light soy sauce
1   Tbs. sherry
1   tsp. cornstarch
1   tsp. vegetable oil
¼   tsp. honey

3   Tbs. vegetable oil
1   clove garlic, minced
2   slices gingerroot, minced
1   medium white onion,
        sliced thin
1   green bell pepper, seeded
        and sliced

PREPARATION
1. Cut steak across the grain
   into thin slices.

2. Combine marinade
   ingredients and mix well.
   Marinate beef for 30 minutes.

COOKING
1. Preheat a wok and add oil.
   When hot, add garlic and
   ginger; stir-fry for a few
   seconds.

2. Add onion and stir-fry for a
   few seconds.

3. Add marinated beef and stir-
   fry for 1 to 2 minutes, or until
   beef is just done.

4. Add green pepper and stir-
   fry for a few seconds. Serve
   hot.

BEEF WITH THREE PEPPERS

1	**pound flank steak, trimmed**

MARINADE

1	**Tbs. vegetable oil**
1	**Tbs. dark soy sauce**
1	**Tbs. sherry**
1	**Tbs. cornstarch**
1	**tsp. honey**

5	**Tbs. vegetable oil**
1	**clove garlic, crushed**
1	**medium onion, cut into thin strips**
1	**dried chili pepper**
1	**green bell pepper, cut into thin strips**
1	**red bell pepper, cut into thin strips**
1	**Tbs. light soy sauce**

PREPARATION

1. Cut steak across grain into ¼-inch-thick slices.

2. Combine marinade ingredients and mix well. Marinate beef for 30 minutes.

COOKING

1. Preheat a wok and add 3 tablespoons oil. When hot, add garlic and stir-fry for a few seconds.

2. Add marinated beef and stir-fry for 4 to 5 minutes, or until beef is just done. Remove and keep warm.

3. Heat the remaining 2 tablespoons oil. Add onion and stir-fry for 30 seconds.

4. Add peppers and soy sauce; stir-fry for 1 minute.

5. Return beef to the wok and mix with peppers. Serve hot.

MINCED BEEF AND BEAN CURD

¼ pound ground
round
1 tsp. light soy sauce
¼ tsp. salt
3 Tbs. vegetable oil
2 cloves garlic, finely
chopped
2 slices gingerroot, finely
chopped
½ cup bamboo shoots,
finely chopped
¼ cup water chestnuts,
finely chopped
3 squares bean curd, cut
into small pieces
1 Tbs. oyster sauce
1 tsp. dark soy sauce
½ tsp. sesame oil
1 scallion, finely chopped

PREPARATION
Season ground beef with light
soy sauce and salt.

COOKING
1. Preheat a wok and add oil.
When hot, add garlic and
ginger; stir-fry until garlic
just starts turning golden
brown.

2. Add ground beef. Stir-fry
over medium heat for 4 to 5
minutes.

3. Add bamboo shoots and
water chestnuts; stir-fry for
1 minute.

4. Add bean curd and stir-fry
for 1 minute.

5. Add oyster sauce, dark soy
sauce, and sesame oil; stir-fry
for a few seconds.

6. Garnish with scallion. Serve
hot.

STEAMED BEEF CAKE

This dish may be cooked in a microwave oven or steamed.

3	dried black mushrooms
½	pound ground beef
1	Tbs. vegetable oil
1	Tbs. cornstarch
2	tsp. light soy sauce
2	tsp. sherry
½	tsp. salt
½	tsp. sugar (optional)
2	Chinese sausages, thinly sliced
½	cup finely chopped water chestnuts

PREPARATION
1. Soak mushrooms in hot water for 15 to 20 minutes, then finely chop.

2. Combine ground beef with oil, cornstarch, soy sauce, sherry, salt, and sugar. Mix well.

3. Combine beef mixture with mushrooms, sausages, and water chestnuts. Shape into a large patty.

COOKING
For microwave: Place beef on a nonmetal dish and cover with plastic wrap. Put in microwave oven and turn dial to high. Cook for 8 minutes.

To steam: Place beef on a heatproof plate in a steamer containing 2 inches of boiling water. Cover and cook over high heat for 10 minutes. Reduce heat and cook an additional 10 minutes.

STEAMED BEEF WITH SZECHUAN CABBAGE TIP

This dish may be cooked in a microwave oven or steamed.

1	pound ground round steak
3	Tbs. canned Szechuan cabbage tip
1	Tbs. vegetable oil
1	Tbs. cornstarch
1	Tbs. sherry
2	tsp. honey
1	tsp. dark soy sauce

PREPARATION
Combine ingredients and mix well.

COOKING
For microwave: Place beef in a nonmetal shallow bowl and cover with plastic wrap. Put the dish inside the microwave oven and turn the dial to high. Cook for 5 to 7 minutes.

To steam: Place beef in a shallow heatproof bowl in a steamer containing 2 inches of boiling water. Cover and cook at high heat for 10 minutes. Reduce heat and cook an additional 10 minutes.

TOMATO BEEF

1   **pound flank steak, trimmed**

MARINADE
1   **Tbs. vegetable oil**
1   **Tbs. dark soy sauce**
1   **tsp. light soy sauce**
1   **tsp. cornstarch**
½   **tsp. red wine**

SAUCE
1   **Tbs. vegetable oil**
1   **medium white onion, coarsely chopped**
1   **cup coarsely chopped green peppers (optional)**
2   **cups tomato wedges**
¼   **cup catsup**

4   **Tbs. vegetable oil**
1   **clove garlic, crushed**
1   **tsp. cornstarch dissolved in 1 Tbs. water**

PREPARATION
1. Cut steak in half lengthwise and slice across the grain into 1½"-×-1"-×-¼" strips.

2. Combine ingredients for marinade and mix well. Marinate beef for 15 minutes.

3. To prepare sauce, preheat a wok or deep skillet and coat the sides and bottom with oil over high heat. Quick-fry the onion. Add green pepper and cook for 1 minute. Add tomatoes and stir-fry for 3 minutes. Add catsup, stir, and pour into a bowl. Set aside.

COOKING
1. Preheat the wok and coat the sides and bottom with oil. When hot, add garlic and stir-fry for a few seconds, then remove the garlic.

2. Add marinated beef, turning to brown uniformly. Cook for 3 to 4 minutes.

3. Add sauce and stir over high heat. Make a well in the center and add the dissolved cornstarch. Stir until thickened. Serve immediately.

SCALLION BEEF

1   **pound flank steak, trimmed**

MARINADE
1   **egg**
1   **Tbs. vegetable oil**
2   **tsp. cornstarch**
1   **tsp. light soy sauce**
½   **tsp. honey**

4   **Tbs. vegetable oil**
2   **slices gingerroot, cut into thin strips**
4   **scallions, cut into 2-inch thin strips**
1   **Tbs. sherry**
1   **Tbs. dark soy sauce**

PREPARATION
1. Cut beef across the grain into thin bite-size pieces.

2. Combine marinade ingredients and mix well. Marinate beef for 30 minutes to 1 hour.

COOKING
1. Preheat a wok and add oil. When hot, add marinated beef and stir-fry for 3 to 4 minutes, or until the beef is just done.

2. Add ginger and scallions and stir-fry for a few seconds.

3 Add sherry and soy sauce and mix well. Serve hot.

BRAISED BEEF AND CHINESE RADISH STEW

2	pounds beef shank or stewing meat
1	pound Chinese white radish, peeled and diagonally sliced
3	Tbs. vegetable oil
2	cloves garlic, crushed
3	slices gingerroot, crushed
¼	cup dark soy sauce
1	Tbs. sherry
2	tsp. honey
1	star anise (optional)
2	cups chicken broth

PREPARATION

1. Cut beef into bite-size pieces.

2. Peel radish. Discard both ends and cut diagonally into 1"-×-2" pieces.

COOKING

1. Preheat oil in a large pot. Add garlic and ginger; stir-fry for a few seconds. Add beef and stir-fry for about 1 minute.

2. Stir in soy sauce, sherry, honey, and star anise. Add chicken broth to cover and bring to a boil. Cover and simmer for 2 hours, leaving a small opening so broth will not boil over.

3. Add radish. Stir and simmer for an additional 30 minutes, until meat is tender. Serve hot.

Makes 6 servings

BITTER MELON AND BEEF

1	**pound flank steak**

MARINADE
2	**Tbs. dark soy sauce**
1	**Tbs. vegetable oil**
1	**tsp. dry sherry**
1	**tsp. honey**
1	**tsp. cornstarch**

2	**Tbs. black bean sauce**
2	**cloves garlic, crushed**
1	**cup peeled and thin-sliced bitter melon**
4	**Tbs. vegetable oil**

PREPARATION

1. Cut steak in half lengthwise, then thin-slice across the grain.

2. Combine marinade ingredients and mix well. Marinate beef for at least 15 minutes while preparing the remaining ingredients.

3. Mix black bean sauce with crushed garlic. Set aside.

4. Bring some water to a boil in a pot, and when it is boiling, turn off heat and submerge the melon slices. Blanch for 1 minute to remove the bitter taste, then discard the water and drain melon on paper towels. Set aside.

COOKING

1. Preheat a wok and add oil. When hot, add the mixture of bean sauce and garlic; stir for several seconds.

2. Add the beef strips, being careful not to stir too much or the beef will get watery. Stir-fry for 1 to 2 minutes, until the separated pieces of beef are brown on both sides.

3. Add the bitter melon. Stir evenly, remove from the heat, and serve hot.

BARBECUED PORK

1	pound pork tenderloin

MARINADE
¼	cup dark soy sauce
3	Tbs. catsup
3	Tbs. hoisin sauce
1	Tbs. cornstarch
1	tsp. honey
1	Tbs. red wine
2	cloves garlic, crushed

PREPARATION
1. Cut pork lengthwise into 2 strips.

2. Combine marinade ingredients and mix well. Marinate the pork at least 4 hours, or overnight.

COOKING
1. Preheat oven to 350°F. Reserving the marinade, place pork strips on the oven rack, with dripping pan underneath. Brush on garlic. After 20 minutes, reduce heat to 300°F and brush both sides of pork with marinade. Barbecue for 20 minutes. Brush both sides of pork again, turn, and barbecue for an additional 15 minutes. Brush remaining marinade over pork, turn, and barbecue a final 15 minutes.

2. Remove from oven. If pork is to be served as an appetizer, cut into thin strips. If main course, cut into 1"-X-2" pieces.

PUNGENT RIBS

This was one of Madame Sun's many delicious recipes.

1½   **pounds spareribs**

MARINADE
2   **Tbs. dark soy sauce**
1   **Tbs. sherry**
1   **tsp. light soy sauce**
¼   **tsp. salt**

2   **Tbs. vegetable oil**
2   **cloves garlic, crushed**
2   **slices gingerroot, crushed**
¼   **cup vinegar**
2   **Tbs. honey**
1   **scallion, chopped**

PREPARATION
1. Cut ribs into 1"-×-1½" pieces.

2. Combine marinade ingredients and mix well. Marinate ribs for about 1 hour.

COOKING
1. Preheat a wok and add oil. When hot, add garlic and ginger; stir-fry for a second or two.

2. Add marinated ribs and stir-fry quickly. Cover and cook on medium heat for 15 minutes.

3. Remove cover. Turn heat higher and stir-fry for 10 to 15 minutes, or until ribs are nicely browned on all sides.

4. Add vinegar and honey; stir-fry for 5 minutes. Discard oil. Garnish with chopped scallion.

LION'S HEAD WITH CABBAGE

A favorite of Madame Sun's and of mine as well.

| 2 | **pounds boned lean pork** |

MARINADE

2	**Tbs. dark soy sauce**
2	**Tbs. cornstarch**
1	**Tbs. sherry**
1	**tsp. light soy sauce**
1	**tsp. honey**

4	**dried black mushrooms**
1	**pound Chinese cabbage**
4	**Tbs. vegetable oil**
1	**tsp. salt**
1	**cup chicken broth**
1	**small onion, chopped**
2	**slices gingerroot, minced**
1	**clove garlic, minced**

PREPARATION

1. Grind pork.

2. Combine marinade ingredients and mix well. Marinate ground pork 15 to 20 minutes, then form into 1½-inch balls.

3. Soak mushrooms in warm water about 15 minutes. Drain, discard stems, and cut into small pieces.

4. Cut Chinese cabbage lengthwise into quarters.

COOKING

1. Preheat oil in a large pot. Add Chinese cabbage and salt. Brown on both sides for 1 minute.

2. Place meatballs on top of Chinese cabbage. Add chicken broth and bring to a boil. Add mushrooms, onion, ginger, and garlic. Cover, reduce heat, and simmer for 1 hour. Serve hot.

Makes 4 to 6 servings

SWEET AND SOUR PORK

1   pound lean pork butt

BATTER
1   cup all-purpose flour
¼   cup cornstarch
¼   tsp. baking powder
¼   tsp. salt
¾   cup water

SAUCE
1   cup reserved pineapple
     juice
¾   cup catsup
¼   cup white vinegar
2   Tbs. honey

1   quart vegetable oil
1   cup thin-sliced green
     pepper
½   cup sliced white onion
1   Tbs. cornstarch
     dissolved in 3 Tbs.
     water
1   cup canned pineapple
     chunks, juice reserved

PREPARATION
1. Cut pork into 1-inch squares.

2. Combine batter ingredients in a bowl, stirring until batter is the consistency of a smooth, thin stream.

3. Blend sauce ingredients in a bowl.

COOKING
1. Heat oil in a kettle until it is very hot (375°F).

2. Dip the pork chunks into the batter, allowing excess to drip off, and gently slip into the hot oil. Deep-fry for 12 minutes, then reduce the heat to medium and deep-fry for an additional 10 minutes. Drain on paper towels and reserve.

3. Preheat a wok or deep skillet and add sauce. Bring to a boil over high heat.

4. Add green pepper and onion, stirring over high heat for 3 minutes.

5. Add the dissolved cornstarch and return to a boil. Stir in pineapple and reserved pork. Serve immediately.

BARBECUED PORK WITH BROCCOLI

½   **pound Barbecued Pork (page 56)**
1   **pound broccoli**
2   **Tbs. vegetable oil**
1   **clove garlic**
½   **tsp. salt**
¼   **cup water or chicken broth**
½   **tsp. sugar**
1½   **tsp. cornstarch dissolved in ¼ cup water**

PREPARATION
1. Slice pork into 1"-×-2" strips.

2. Cut broccoli into 3-inch pieces from top of floret to stem. Peel stems and cut away leaves.

COOKING
1. Preheat a wok or deep skillet and coat bottom and sides with oil. Rub with garlic and discard.

2. Add salt, then broccoli, and stir-fry for 1 minute.

3. Add water or broth and sugar. Cover and cook over high heat for 5 minutes.

4. With slotted spoon, remove broccoli to a serving dish. Add dissolved cornstarch to the liquid remaining in the wok and allow to thicken. Add pork and stir-fry for 1 minute.

5. Spoon meat and sauce over the broccoli. Serve hot.

BRAISED PORK LEG WITH BRUSSELS SPROUTS

3 to 4 pounds fresh pork
30   Brussels sprouts
1   cup water
¼   cup dark soy sauce
1   Tbs. light soy sauce
1   Tbs. sherry
1   Tbs. honey
2   slices gingerroot
2   cloves garlic

PREPARATION
1. Trim pork of fat.

2. Wash and trim any flawed outer leaves and end of the stem from Brussels sprouts.

COOKING
1. Combine remaining ingredients in a large pot. Bring to a boil and add pork. Cover and simmer for 2 to 3 hours, or until the pork is tender. (Add water if necessary.)

2. Remove pork from pot and keep warm.

3. Add Brussels sprouts to pot. Cover and cook over medium heat for 10 to 15 minutes, or until tender. Serve pork surrounded with Brussels sprouts.

Makes 6 servings

BRAISED PORK WITH CHINESE MUSHROOMS

10	dried black mushrooms
1	cup hot water
1	pound pork butt
2	Tbs. dark soy sauce
1	tsp. light soy sauce
½	tsp. honey
2	slices gingerroot
1	clove garlic
3	Tbs. vegetable oil
1	cup chicken broth

PREPARATION

1. Soak mushrooms in hot water for 30 minutes. Drain and reserve liquid.

2. Cut pork butt into large pieces.

3. Mix soy sauces and honey.

4. Crush ginger and garlic.

COOKING

1. Preheat a wok and add oil. When hot, drop in ginger and garlic; stir-fry for a few seconds.

2. Add pork and mushrooms. Stir-fry for 1 to 2 minutes.

3. Add soy sauce mixture and stir-fry for 1 minute.

4. Add chicken broth and reserved mushroom liquid. Bring to a boil, cover, and simmer over low heat for 1 hour, or until pork is tender.

5. Serve pork topped by mushrooms, stem side down, in uniform arrangement.

MU SHU PORK IN PANCAKE ROLLS

Each guest spreads a pancake with a little hoisin sauce and about 3 tablespoons of filling. The pancake is then rolled and eaten.

½   cup thin strips of pork
1   tsp. light soy sauce
½   tsp. sugar
¼   tsp. sherry
¼   tsp. salt
¼   cup dried black
     mushrooms
1   Tbs. diced cloud ears
     (optional)

EGG STRIPS
2   small eggs
1   Tbs. vegetable oil

PANCAKES
2   cups all-purpose flour
¼   cup cornstarch
3   cups water
4   egg whites
¼   cup vegetable oil

4   Tbs. vegetable oil
1   Tbs. dark soy
     sauce
½   pound any white
     cabbage, sliced thin
¼   cup canned sliced
     bamboo shoots
hoisin sauce for serving

Note: Beef or chicken can be substituted for the pork.

PREPARATION
1. Combine pork with light soy sauce, sugar, sherry, and salt.

2. Soak mushrooms in warm water for 20 minutes. Cut off and discard stems. Thin-slice mushrooms.

3. Soak cloud ears in warm water for 5 to 10 minutes. Wash and drain.

4. To prepare egg strips, beat the eggs then heat the oil in a skillet. Pour in eggs and fry on both sides to make a thin pancake. Cut into thin strips and reserve.

5. In a bowl, combine ingredients for pancakes and beat with a wire whisk. Strain batter into another bowl. Lightly oil an 8-inch crepe pan or nonstick skillet. Place over medium heat. Pour in about ¼ cup batter, rolling pan to spread evenly. Cook until dry (do not brown), turn, and cook for a few seconds. Repeat until all batter is used. Keep pancakes warm.

COOKING
1. Preheat a wok and add oil. When hot, add pork and dark soy sauce. Stir-fry for 4 to 5 minutes.

2. Add cabbage and stir-fry for 1 minute.

3. Add mushrooms, cloud ears, and bamboo shoots; stir-fry for a few seconds. Cover and cook over low heat for 1 minute.

4. Remove cover, add egg strips, and stir-fry for a few seconds. Place in a dish and serve accompanied with pancakes and a small bowl of hoisin sauce.

PORK WITH BEAN SPROUTS

1	pound lean pork
1	tsp. cornstarch
1	Tbs. light soy sauce
1	tsp. sherry
½	tsp. sesame oil
3	Tbs. vegetable oil
1	clove garlic, crushed
1	slice gingerroot, crushed
1	pound bean sprouts, trimmed

PREPARATION
Cut pork into thin strips. In a bowl combine cornstarch, soy sauce, sherry, and sesame oil. Mix well. Add pork.

COOKING
1. Preheat a wok or deep skillet and add oil. When hot, add garlic and ginger; stir-fry for a few seconds.

2. Add pork and soy sauce mixture. Stir-fry for 4 to 5 minutes over medium heat.

3. Add bean sprouts and stir-fry for 2 minutes. Serve hot.

PORK WITH GREEN AND RED PEPPERS

1	**pound lean pork**

MARINADE
1	**Tbs. dark soy sauce**
1	**Tbs. cornstarch**
1	**tsp. red wine**
1	**tsp. vegetable oil**
¼	**tsp. sugar**

4	**Tbs. vegetable oil**
1	**tsp. light soy sauce**
1	**cup thin-sliced green pepper**
¼	**cup thin-sliced red pepper**
3	**scallions, cut into 2-inch lengths**
¼	**tsp. salt**

PREPARATION
1. Cut pork into ½"-×-2" strips.

2. Combine marinade ingredients and mix well. Marinate pork for 20 minutes.

COOKING
1. Preheat a wok, and swirl oil around it.

2. Add pork and light soy sauce; stir-fry for 5 to 10 minutes.

3. Add peppers, scallions, and salt; stir-fry for 2 minutes. Serve hot.

PORK WITH EGGPLANT IN HOT SAUCE

½	cup minced pork
1	pound eggplant
	(preferably Chinese)
3	Tbs. vegetable oil
2	slices gingerroot, minced
1	clove garlic, minced
1	Tbs. hot sauce
1	tsp. dark soy sauce
1	tsp. light soy sauce
½	cup chicken broth
dash black pepper
½	Tbs. cider vinegar
1	tsp. sesame oil
1	scallion, finely chopped

PREPARATION
Wash eggplant. Cut off and discard both ends. Cut into ½"-×-2" pieces.

COOKING
1. Preheat the wok and add oil. When hot, add ginger and garlic and stir-fry for a few seconds.

2. Add minced pork and stir-fry for 2 minutes.

3. Add eggplant and stir-fry over medium heat until soft.

4. Add hot sauce, soy sauces, and chicken broth. Gently mash eggplant to absorb ingredients. Stir-fry for 1 minute.

5. Add black pepper and vinegar; stir-fry to blend.

6. Garnish with sesame oil and chopped scallion.

PORK WITH BEAN CURD, SZECHUAN STYLE

MARINADE
1   Tbs. hoisin sauce
1   tsp. light soy sauce
1   tsp. cornstarch blended
      with 1 tsp. water

½   pound ground lean pork
3   Tbs. vegetable oil
1   slice gingerroot
3   squares bean curd, cut
      into ½-inch cubes
2   Tbs. dark soy sauce
1   Tbs. chili paste with
      garlic
½   tsp. honey

PREPARATION
1. Combine marinade
   ingredients.

2. Add the pork to the marinade
   and marinate for 20 to 30
   minutes.

COOKING
1. Preheat a wok and add oil.
   Swirl ginger slice in wok and
   discard.

2. Add marinated pork and stir-
   fry for 5 to 10 minutes, or
   until the pork is done.

3. Add bean curd, and press
   them down gently as you stir.

4. Add the remaining
   ingredients and stir in well.
   Cook for an additional 2
   minutes. Serve hot.

PORK-STUFFED FUZZY MELONS

Another recipe in Madame Sun Yat-sen's collection of favorites. While instructions are given for preparing in a microwave oven, this dish may also be cooked in a steamer.

½ pound lean pork
6 medium dried black mushrooms soaked in warm water
⅓ cup bamboo shoots
5 water chestnuts
1 Tbs. cornstarch
1 tsp. light soy sauce
1 tsp. sesame oil
½ tsp. sugar
¼ tsp. salt
⅛ tsp. white pepper
3 fuzzy melons (about 14 ounces each)

SAUCE
¾ cup water
1 Tbs. sherry
½ tsp. dark soy sauce
½ tsp. sugar
½ tsp. salt
½ tsp. cornstarch dissolved in 1 Tbs. water
¼ tsp. sesame oil
dash white pepper

2 Tbs. vegetable oil

PREPARATION
1. In a grinder or food processor grind pork, mushrooms, bamboo shoots, and water chestnuts.

2. Combine ground mixture with cornstarch, soy sauce, sesame oil, sugar, salt, and white pepper.

3. Peel fuzzy melons, and cut off ends. Scoop out seeds, making a hollow running the length of each melon. Fill with pork stuffing.

4. Combine sauce ingredients. Stir well.

COOKING
1. Preheat a wok and add oil. When hot, roll stuffed melons on all sides until golden brown.

2. Place melons in a deep, nonmetal heatproof dish and pour the sauce over them.

3. Cover with plastic wrap and place in a microwave oven. Turn dial to high for 15 to 20 minutes. Serve immediately.

ENTRÉES

Poultry	雞鴨類	(Chicken)

CHICKEN VELVET AND GREEN PEAS

2   **chicken breasts**

MARINADE
3   **pieces gingerroot, finely chopped**
2   **scallions, finely chopped**
1   **Tbs. sherry**
2   **tsp. light soy sauce**
2   **Tbs. cornstarch**
dash white pepper

6   **egg whites**
5   **Tbs. vegetable oil**
½   **cup fresh or frozen green peas**
½   **cup finely chopped cooked ham**

PREPARATION
1. Finely mince chicken breasts.

2. Combine marinade ingredients and mix well. Stir in minced chicken and marinate for 15 minutes.

3. Whip egg whites until stiff. Fold into marinated chicken.

COOKING
1. Preheat a wok and add oil. When hot, add marinated chicken and stir-fry vigorously for 2 to 3 minutes.

2. Add green peas and stir-fry with chicken a few seconds.

3. Place on platter and garnish with ham.

SHREDDED CHICKEN SALAD

When I was a young girl in a Chinese boarding school, all my schoolmates had pictures of their favorite movie stars pinned to the dormitory walls. Of course, I was no exception, and my favorite was Cary Grant.

Believe it or not, when I opened my restaurant, many years later, Cary Grant was among my first customers. We became friends over the years, and I think I am the only girl from that school who ended up actually meeting the idol whose photo was tacked to those dormitory walls! This recipe is Cary Grant's favorite, as well as one of the most popular dishes in the restaurant.

2	chicken breasts or 2 drumsticks
2	quarts vegetable oil
⅓	package rice noodles
6	won ton wrappers, cut in ⅛-inch strips
2	Tbs. finely chopped toasted almonds
2	scallions, white parts only, sliced thin
1	Tbs. light soy sauce
1	tsp. sesame oil
1	tsp. mustard paste
¼	tsp. five-spice powder (optional)
½	head lettuce, shredded

PREPARATION
1. Put chicken in a pot, cover with water, and bring to a boil. Reduce heat and simmer for 20 minutes. Remove and drain on paper towels.

COOKING

1. Preheat a wok, add oil, and heat to 350°F. (Test for readiness by dropping one strand of rice noodle in oil. If it sinks to bottom, oil is not hot enough. If it pops up immediately, oil is ready.)

2. Divide noodles into 3 parts and deep-fry separately. Noodles will "explode" in contact with oil. Remove at once before oil is absorbed by noodles. Drain on paper towels.

3. Deep-fry won ton strips until crispy brown. Drain on paper towels.

4. Deep-fry chicken for 5 minutes. Drain on paper towels. Bone and cut chicken into strips, skin and all. (You should have about 2 cups.)

5. Toss chicken meat in a large bowl with almonds, scallions, soy sauce, sesame oil, mustard paste, and five-spice powder.

6. Add won ton strips and noodles. Mix thoroughly. (Do not toss or salad will become soggy.)

7. Place lettuce on a platter and top with chicken. Serve.

CHESTNUT CHICKEN

1	chicken, boned
1	pound fresh chestnuts, or ½ pound dried chestnuts

SAUCE

2	Tbs. sherry
1	Tbs. light soy sauce
2	tsp. sugar
1	tsp. salt

4	Tbs. vegetable oil
1	scallion, cut into ½-inch pieces
3	slices gingerroot
½	cup chicken broth

PREPARATION

1. Cut chicken into bite-size pieces.

2. Peel and skin fresh chestnuts and soak for 15 minutes in hot water. If using dried chestnuts, soak for 1 hour.

3. Combine sauce ingredients.

COOKING

1. Preheat a wok, add oil, and heat to boiling. Add scallion and ginger; stir-fry for a few seconds.

2. Add chicken and stir-fry for 2 to 3 minutes.

3. Add chestnuts and chicken broth. Stir well.

4. Add sauce and bring to a boil. Reduce heat and simmer for 30 minutes, or until chicken and chestnuts are tender. Serve hot.

WALNUT CHICKEN

1   **medium chicken, boned**

MARINADE
1   **Tbs. dark soy sauce**
1   **tsp. light soy sauce**
1   **tsp. sherry**
½   **tsp. honey**
½   **tsp. sesame oil**
2   **tsp. cornstarch**

½   **cup halved walnuts**
3   **cups vegetable oil**
1   **scallion, finely chopped**

PREPARATION
1. Cut chicken into bite-size pieces.

2. Combine marinade ingredients and mix well. Marinate chicken for 15 to 20 minutes.

3. Soak walnuts in boiling water for 10 minutes, or until the skins come off easily; peel. Dry walnuts briefly on a paper towel in the oven.

COOKING
1. Preheat a wok, add oil, and heat to 325°F. Deep-fry walnuts until golden brown, about 1 minute. (Be careful not to burn them.) Remove, drain on paper towels, and set aside.

2. Drain all but 3 tablespoons oil from wok. Heat and add chicken; stir-fry for 2 to 3 minutes.

3. Add walnuts and stir-fry briefly. Add scallion and mix well. Serve hot.

CHICKEN, VEGETABLES, AND MUSHROOMS

½	cup canned or homemade chicken broth
½	cup sliced celery
½	cup sliced Chinese white cabbage
2	chicken breasts, sliced
1	slice gingerroot, diced
1	scallion, sliced
½	cup mushrooms
½	cup sliced water chestnuts
½	cup Chinese pea pods
1	tsp. cornstarch dissolved in 1 Tbs. water

COOKING

1. In a preheated wok or large saucepan, bring chicken broth to a boil. Add celery and Chinese cabbage. Cook for 3 to 5 minutes.

2. Add chicken, ginger, and scallion. Mix well and cook for 3 to 4 minutes, or until chicken is just done.

3. Add mushrooms, water chestnuts, and pea pods. Stir well.

4. Make a hole in the center by removing the ingredients to the edges. Pour in the cornstarch and mix well with the juice, cooking until it thickens. Serve hot.

CHICKEN IN OYSTER SAUCE

1½ pounds boned chicken

MARINADE
1 Tbs. sherry
1 Tbs. dark soy sauce
1 tsp. light soy sauce
2 tsp. cornstarch
1 tsp. sugar (optional)
pinch black pepper

OYSTER SAUCE
3 Tbs. oyster sauce
1 Tbs. sherry
1 tsp. light soy sauce
1 tsp. sesame oil
1 tsp. cornstarch

3 Tbs. vegetable oil
2 cloves garlic, finely chopped
1 slice gingerroot, finely chopped

PREPARATION
1. Cut chicken into 3"-×-2" strips.

2. Combine marinade ingredients and mix well. Marinate chicken for 15 minutes.

3. Combine ingredients for oyster sauce in a small bowl.

COOKING
1. Preheat a wok and add oil. When hot, brown both sides of each piece of chicken and cook until done.

2. Add garlic and ginger; stir-fry for a few seconds. Bring to a boil.

3. Add oyster sauce. Stir-fry evenly for 1 minute. Serve hot.

IMPERIAL CHICKEN

One of Madame Sun's recipes.

1   pound boned chicken

MARINADE
1   Tbs. dark soy sauce
1   Tbs. honey
1   Tbs. red wine
1   Tbs. vinegar
½   tsp. sesame oil
1½   tsp. cornstarch

2   Tbs. vegetable oil
1   clove garlic, crushed
6   leaves butter lettuce

PREPARATION
1. Cut chicken into ½-inch cubes.

2. Combine marinade ingredients and mix well. Marinate chicken for at least 1 hour. Drain and reserve marinade.

COOKING
1. Preheat a wok and add oil over high heat (375°F). Add chicken, reduce heat to medium (350°F), and stir-fry 3 to 4 minutes, or until chicken browns.

2. Remove chicken with slotted spoon.

3. Pour out most of the oil. Reheat and add garlic.

4. Return chicken to the wok and add marinade; stir-fry for 2 minutes.

5. Serve chicken surrounded by lettuce leaves.

PEASANT-STYLE STEWED CHICKEN

1	2-pound chicken
2	Tbs. dark soy sauce

SAUCE

1	ounce tiger lily flowers
½	ounce cloud ears
4	dried black mushrooms
¼	cup sliced bamboo shoots
3	Tbs. dark soy sauce
1	Tbs. sherry
1	tsp. honey
1	tsp. salt
⅛	tsp. pepper

5	cups vegetable oil
2	scallions, sliced
2	slices gingerroot, sliced
1	Tbs. cornstarch dissolved in ¼ cup water

PREPARATION

1. Clean and dry chicken. Rub inside and outside with soy sauce.

2. Prepare sauce: Soak lily flowers, cloud ears, and mushrooms in hot water for 15 minutes. Drain. Trim off ends of lily flowers. Cut mushrooms in half. Combine all ingredients and mix well.

COOKING

1. Preheat wok and add oil. When hot, deep-fry chicken for 3 to 4 minutes, or until golden brown. Remove from wok and drain oil.

2. Return 3 tablespoons oil to wok and heat. Add scallions and ginger and stir-fry for a few seconds.

3. Add sauce. Return chicken to wok and spoon sauce over it. Cover and stew over medium heat (325°F) 20 to 24 minutes, turning chicken several times.

4. Remove chicken and cut into bite-size pieces. Place chicken pieces on a large serving platter. Using slotted spoon, place remaining ingredients on top of chicken.

5. Remove about 3 to 4 tablespoons of sauce from wok and combine with dissolved cornstarch. Pour into wok and mix well. Turn heat high (375°F) and bring to a boil while stirring. Pour thickened sauce over chicken. Serve hot.

Makes 6 to 8 servings

CHINESE SAUSAGES WITH CHICKEN

This dish and the following one can be cooked in a steamer or a microwave oven.

2   cups boned chicken
        breast, cut in strips
1   Tbs. water
1   tsp. vegetable oil
1   tsp. light soy sauce
1   tsp. cornstarch
1   tsp. honey
½   cup diagonally thin-
        sliced Chinese
        sausages

PREPARATION
1. In a heatproof glass bowl combine chicken with the water, oil, soy sauce, cornstarch, and honey. Stir and flatten surface.

2. Place sausage slices neatly on top of chicken.

COOKING
To steam: Place bowl in a steamer containing 2 inches of boiling water. Cover and cook at high heat for 15 minutes. Reduce heat and cook an additional 15 minutes.

    For microwave: Cover bowl with plastic wrap and place in a microwave oven. Turn dial on high and set cooking time for 10 minutes. If you want well-done chicken, cook for 15 minutes.

STEAMED CHICKEN WITH CHINESE MUSHROOMS

2　boned chicken breasts

MARINADE
1　Tbs. light soy sauce
1　Tbs. vegetable oil
2　tsp. cornstarch
1　tsp. honey
1　tsp. sherry

10　medium-size dried black
　　mushrooms
5　slices gingerroot
1　scallion

PREPARATION
1. Cut chicken into bite-size pieces.

2. Combine marinade ingredients and mix well. Marinate chicken for about 15 minutes.

3. Soak mushrooms in cold water for an hour, or until tender. Cut into halves.

4. Cut ginger into very thin strips.

5. Cut scallion into 1-inch pieces, then into very thin strips.

6. Place the marinated chicken in a shallow heatproof glass bowl. Mix in the mushrooms, ginger, and scallion.

COOKING
For microwave: Cover the bowl firmly with plastic wrap, but not sealed too tightly. Place chicken in the microwave, turn dial to high and set cooking time to 8 minutes. (If you like your chicken well done, set dial for 10 minutes.)

　　To steam: Place bowl in a steamer containing 2 inches of boiling water. Cover and cook at high heat for 15 minutes. Reduce heat and cook for an additional 15 minutes.

"FOUR-JEWEL" IN CHICKEN

This was one of Madame Sun's favorite recipes.

2   chicken breasts

MARINADE
1   Tbs. vegetable oil
1   Tbs. water
1½   tsp. cornstarch
1   tsp. honey
1   tsp. light soy sauce
1   tsp. rice wine or white
           wine

3   Tbs. vegetable oil
1   slice gingerroot, finely
           chopped
1   scallion, finely chopped
6   small Chinese white
           cabbages, hearts only

12   fresh or canned
           asparagus spears, cut
           into 2-inch lengths
½   cup chicken broth
½   can straw mushrooms,
           rinsed and drained
½   can whole bamboo
           shoots, rinsed and cut
           into halves
1½   tsp. cornstarch dissolved
           in 1 Tbs. chicken broth

PREPARATION
1. Cut chicken into 1"-×-2"
   strips

2. Combine marinade
   ingredients and mix well.
   Marinate chicken for 30
   minutes.

COOKING
1. Preheat a wok, add oil, and
   heat to very hot (375°F). Add
   ginger and scallion; stir-fry
   for a few seconds.

2. Add chicken and stir-fry for
   5 minutes.
3. Add Chinese cabbage hearts,
   asparagus, and chicken broth;
   stir-fry for 2 minutes.

4. Add mushrooms and bamboo
   shoots; cook for 1 minute.

5. Add dissolved cornstarch,
   mix well, and cook until
   sauce thickens.

6. Place chicken in center of
   platter and arrange other
   ingredients around it. Serve.

Note: Broccoli may be substituted for
the Chinese cabbage.

LEMON CHICKEN

1   **boned chicken breast**
salt

BATTER
½   **cup all-purpose flour**
¼   **cup cornstarch**
½   **tsp. baking powder**
¼   **tsp. salt**
¾   **cup water**
½   **tsp. vegetable oil**

SAUCE
½   **cup water**
3   **Tbs. fresh lemon juice**
2   **Tbs. honey**
1   **tsp. cornstarch dissolved**
      in 2 Tbs. water

1   **quart vegetable oil**
1   **tsp. cornstarch dissolved**
      in 2 Tbs. water

GARNISH
lemon slices, halved
Maraschino cherries

PREPARATION
1. Thin-slice chicken into 4 pieces. Salt pieces.

2. Combine batter ingredients and stir until smooth and the consistency of a ribbon stream.

3. Combine ingredients for sauce.

COOKING
1. Heat oil in a wide-based, deep-sided skillet until it is very hot (375°F).

2. Dip each piece of chicken into the batter and let the excess drip back. Slip into the hot oil, deep-frying one piece at a time for about 5 minutes. The oil must remain hot so that each piece of chicken becomes crisp and not soggy. Remove, drain on paper towels, and set aside.

3. Pour sauce into a wok and bring to a boil.

4. Add dissolved cornstarch and stir over heat until the mixture thickens.

SERVING

1. Arrange the 4 pieces of chicken in the center of a platter.

2. Cut each piece into 5 smaller pieces, but fit back together to retain the shape of each original piece. Pour the hot lemon sauce over the chicken.

3. Arrange the lemon slices around the border of the platter. Place a cherry on each lemon slice. Serve immediately to maintain crispness of the chicken.

SAUTÉED CHICKEN WINGS

8	chicken wings
3	Tbs. vegetable oil
2	cloves garlic, crushed
3	Tbs. oyster sauce
2	Tbs. dark soy sauce
1	tsp. light soy sauce
1	cup chicken broth
1	Tbs. honey

PREPARATION
Divide each wing at the joints into three parts. Wash and dry with paper towels.

COOKING
1. Preheat a wok or deep skillet and add the oil, swirling to coat the wok.

2. Swish garlic around wok, discarding when it turns black.

3. Add the 2 large parts of each wing and brown on both sides, then brown the wing tips.

4. Mix the oyster sauce and soy sauces into the chicken.

5. Stir in the chicken broth and honey. Cover and cook over medium heat 20 minutes. Stir occasionally to prevent sticking. Serve hot.

VERMICELLI CHICKEN

½   pound vermicelli

MARINADE
1   Tbs. vegetable oil
1   Tbs. dark soy sauce
1   tsp. light soy sauce
1   tsp. cornstarch

1   cup thin-sliced chicken
½   cup dried black
      mushrooms
3   Tbs. vegetable oil
1   clove garlic
1   cup thin-sliced Chinese
      white cabbage
½   cup canned sliced
      bamboo shoots, rinsed
3   cups chicken broth
½   cup thin-sliced Chinese
      pea pods
¼   cup thin-sliced scallions

PREPARATION
1. Soak vermicelli in warm water to cover for 30 minutes. Drain off water. Using scissors, cut vermicelli into 4-inch lengths.

2. Combine ingredients for marinade and mix well. Marinate chicken for 30 minutes.

3. Soak black mushrooms in hot water for about 15 minutes. Clean and discard stems.

COOKING
1. Preheat a wok or deep skillet (350°F). Add the oil, swirling to coat the wok. Swish garlic clove around wok for a few seconds, and discard.

2. Add marinated chicken. Quick-fry over high heat (375°F) for 3 minutes.

3. Add black mushrooms and stir-fry for 1 minute.

4. Add cabbage and stir-fry for 2 minutes.

5. Add bamboo shoots and chicken broth. Cover and bring to a boil.

6. Add vermicelli and stir well. Cover and cook 3 minutes.

7. Add pea pods and stir-fry for 1 minute.

8. Turn into serving dish and garnish with scallions. Serve immediately.

Makes 4 to 6 servings

CHICKEN WITH CASHEWS

MARINADE
1½   tsp. vegetable oil
1   tsp. light soy sauce
½   tsp. honey
½   tsp. water
1   tsp. cornstarch

1   cup sliced chicken breast
2   Tbs. vegetable oil
1   clove garlic, crushed
½   cup pea pods
½   cup button mushrooms
½   cup sliced bamboo
       shoots
¼   cup chicken broth
½   cup raw cashew nuts

PREPARATION
Combine marinade ingredients and mix well. Marinate chicken for 30 minutes.

COOKING
1. Preheat a wok or deep skillet and add oil. When hot, stir around garlic, remove, and discard.

2. Add chicken and stir-fry for 3 minutes.

3. Add pea pods, mushrooms, bamboo shoots, and chicken broth. Stir-fry for 1 minute.

4. Add cashew nuts and stir-fry for 1 minute. Serve immediately.

SWEET AND SOUR CHICKEN

1   pound skinned and
     boned chicken breast

BATTER
½   cup all-purpose flour
¼   cup cornstarch
½   tsp. baking powder
¼   tsp. salt
¾   cup water

SAUCE
¾   cup catsup
¼   cup white vinegar
3   Tbs. sugar
1   cup reserved pineapple
     juice

2   quarts vegetable oil
½   cup chopped white onion
½   cup chopped green
     pepper

1   Tbs. cornstarch
     dissolved in 2 Tbs.
     water
1   cup canned pineapple
     chunks (reserve juice)

PREPARATION
1. Cut chicken breast into 1-
   inch pieces.

2. In a bowl, combine dry
   ingredients for batter. Add
   water and stir until batter is
   the consistency of a smooth,
   thin stream.

3. Combine sauce ingredients
   and stir well.

COOKING
1. Heat vegetable oil in a large
   kettle to 375°F.

2. Dip chicken pieces into
   batter, letting excess batter
   drip back into the bowl. Slip
   chicken pieces into the hot
   oil, a few at a time, and deep-
   fry for 5 minutes. Drain on
   paper towels and set aside.

3. Preheat a wok or deep skillet
   and add sauce. Bring to a boil
   over high heat.

4. Add onion and green pepper.
   Return to a boil.

5. Stir in the dissolved
   cornstarch and add pineapple
   chunks.

6. When the mixtures boils, add
   chicken. Stir well and serve
   immediately.

CHICKEN, HAM, AND GREENS

This very famous Cantonese dish is served mostly at banquets.

SAUCE
¼	cup chicken broth
1	Tbs. vegetable oil
2	tsp. sherry
½	tsp. cornstarch

24	1¼"-✕-2" pieces cooked Virginia ham
1	2- to 3-pound chicken
1	tsp. salt
1	pound broccoli, stems trimmed
2	Tbs. vegetable oil
2	slices gingerroot
1	tsp. sugar
2 to 3 Tbs. chicken broth

PREPARATION
In a small bowl, combine sauce ingredients

COOKING
1. Steam ham for 10 minutes. Keep warm.

2. In a large pot, boil enough water or chicken broth to cover chicken. Add chicken and ½ teaspoon salt and simmer for 5 minutes. Reduce heat to low and cook for 15 to 20 minutes. (If you prefer well-done chicken, let stand an additional 5 minutes.) Set aside to cool.

3. Thin-slice cold chicken into 24 pieces the same size as the ham. Arrange on a large serving platter alternately with the ham.

4. Fill a wok or deep skillet with water and bring to a boil. Blanch broccoli for 2 minutes. Wash with cold water and drain.

5. Heat the oil in the wok. Add ginger and stir-fry for a few seconds. Add broccoli, sugar, ½ teaspoon salt, and chicken broth. Stir-fry for 1 minute, or until broccoli is just tender. Arrange around chicken and ham.

6. Heat sauce ingredients in the wok. Stir until mixture thickens. Pour over chicken and ham.

Makes 6 servings

ENTRÉES

Poultry	雞鴨類	(Duck)

Duck was a delicacy in old China, where it was a preferred food of wealthy landlords and the nobility. Wishing to achieve the success and power of the rich by eating what the privileged ate, the common people made duck a special food. The dishes often assumed the name of the provincial capital from which they originated, for it was around the capitals that the powerful lived. Hence, Peking Duck, Nanking Duck, and Szechuan Duck.

The most famous and internationally popular of these dishes is, of course, Peking (or Beijing) Duck, originally prepared by the chefs of Peking for the Emperor and his court. Peking Duck is eaten with plum sauce placed in a thin pancake, which is rolled with slivers of spring onions for flavor. Usually only the crisp skin is eaten, as this is considered to be the choicest part of the duck. No one will disagree with you, however, if you want to eat the meat as well in your next helping! The preparation is time consuming, but a recipe has been included in this section.

The famous Szechuan Duck is eaten with a small yeast roll and a special piquant duck sauce not unlike plum sauce. The roll and crisp duck go so well together, perked by the flavor of the sauce, that it is impossible to count those calories!

Nanking Duck comes from the old capital of China and is a salted duck delicacy.

Another delicious duck dish, from Hangchow, is called Westlake Duck. Boned and slow-steamed for hours, it is so tender that it falls apart with the slightest touch of a chopstick.

Eight Precious Duck originates in Shanghai and is for Chinese New Year what turkey is for an American Thanksgiving. It is usually the most extravagant food offering made to dead ancestors just before sitting down to the family New Year's meal. Wealthier homes have several Eight Precious Ducks, some used as offerings, others used for themselves, while the less wealthy families eventually eat the duck used as the offering. Its name comes from its stuffing, made with eight different precious and delicious ingredients. You are sure to find Eight Precious Duck among your favorite poultry dishes.

EGG-GARNISHED DUCK

Madame Sun particularly liked this recipe because it is so unusual.

1	2½- to 3-pound duck
1	Tbs. salt
¼	tsp. pepper
2	Tbs. dark soy sauce
1	Tbs. honey (optional)
2	quarts vegetable oil
1	Tbs. red wine
½	cup chicken broth
2	cups water
2	Tbs. cornstarch dissolved in 2 Tbs. water
6	eggs, hard-boiled and cut into 6 wedges each
1	bunch parsley

PREPARATION

1. Clean the duck carefully inside and out.

2. Rub with salt, pepper, and 1 tablespoon dark soy sauce. If you prefer a sweet taste, rub on the honey.

COOKING

1. Heat oil in a roaster and when it is hot (about 350°F), put in the duck and deep-fry for 10 to 15 minutes, turning it so that it browns evenly. Drain and clean the roaster and return the duck to it.

2. To make a sauce, blend together cooking wine, 1 tablespoon dark soy sauce, the chicken broth, and 2 cups of water. After you have removed the oil from the roaster, pour this blend over the duck.

3. Place the roaster on 2 burners on top of the stove and cook over medium heat until the liquid comes to a boil. Reduce heat to medium-low and cook for 2 hours.

4. Remove the duck to a serving platter. Stir the dissolved cornstarch into the roaster and cook until the sauce is thick (about 1 minute).

5. Pour the hot sauce over the duck and garnish duck with wedges of hard-boiled egg. Place parsley sprigs between the egg wedges.

Makes 4 to 6 servings

LICHEE DUCK

1   **3-pound duck**

MARINADE
¼   **cup light soy sauce**
1   **Tbs. sherry**
3   **slices gingerroot, minced**
1   **Tbs. cornstarch**

SAUCE
½   **cup reserved juice from**
    lichees
1   **Tbs. light soy sauce**
2   **tsp. cornstarch**

4   **Tbs. vegetable oil**
½   **cup chicken broth**
½   **reserved juice from**
    lichees
1   **cup canned lichees, juice**
    reserved
2   **scallions, finely chopped**

PREPARATION
1. Cut duck into bite-size pieces.

2. Combine marinade ingredients and mix well. Marinate duck for an hour.

3. Mix sauce ingredients.

COOKING
1. Preheat a wok and add oil. When hot, add duck and stir-fry for 2 to 3 minutes. Drain fat.

2. Add chicken broth and ½ cup lichee juice. Bring to a boil, reduce heat, and simmer for 30 minutes, or until duck is tender.

3. Add lichees and stir-fry for 30 seconds, or until fruit is heated through.

4. Add sauce and bring to a boil. Stir until thickened.

5. Sprinkle with scallions.

Makes 4 to 6 servings

BEIJING (PEKING) DUCK

Ever since President Nixon opened the door to China, my restaurant has had thousands of requests for Beijing Duck—even though we need 2 days' prior notice.

1	3- to 4-pound freshly killed duck
1	tsp. salt
2	scallions, stems tied in a knot
2	slices gingerroot
1	quart water
3	tsp. honey
2	Tbs. cornstarch dissolved in 4 Tbs. water
1	can oven-ready biscuits
6	scallions, cut diagonally into 2-inch pieces
1	small can plum sauce

lemon slices
parsley sprigs

PREPARATION

1. Clean duck inside and out, and dry thoroughly. Salt lightly inside and out.

2. Stuff duck with scallions and ginger.

3. Stitch the tail vent closed with a length of fine wire. Attach another wire to the neck as a handle.

4. Mix the water and honey in a large wok or a small roasting pan and bring to a boil. When boiling, stir in the dissolved cornstarch and continue boiling, stirring until the liquid has the consistency of a thin stream.

5. Reduce heat. Holding the duck by the neck wire, dip into the liquid mixture 3 or

4 times to coat the duck completely on all sides.

6. Remove duck, hang overnight in a cool place, preferably with an electric fan to dry the skin thoroughly.

COOKING

1. Preheat oven to 400°F. Place duck, breast side up, on a flat rack in a roasting pan and roast for 30 minutes. Turn the duck over, reduce heat to 300°F, and roast for an additional 30 minutes. Return the duck to breast-up position and roast a final 15 to 20 minutes.

2. Divide each oven-ready biscuit in half. In the bottom of a steamer, bring 2 inches of water to a boil. Put the biscuits in the steaming section, cover, and steam for 5 minutes.

SERVING

1. Divide the scallion pieces on a butter plate for each diner and put 1 tablespoon plum sauce on each plate.

2. Remove the drumsticks and wings from the duck. Carefully slice off all skin into 1"-×-2" pieces and lay them aside. Slice the meat from the bone. Place all the carved meat on a serving platter, and cover with skin pieces. Place the wings and drumsticks in their relative positions to make the presentation look like a whole duck. Surround the duck with alternate slices of lemon and sprigs of parsley.

EATING

Split a biscuit in half. On one half, place the scallion, plum sauce, duck, and skin. Cover with the top half of biscuit and eat like a sandwich.

Makes 4 to 6 servings

BRAISED DUCK IN PLUM SAUCE

1	2- to 3-pound duck
¼	cup plum sauce
2	slices gingerroot, crushed
2	cloves garlic, crushed
2	Tbs. brown bean sauce
4	Tbs. honey
1	Tbs. dark soy sauce
4	Tbs. vegetable oil
2	tsp. cornstarch dissolved in 2 Tbs. water

salt to taste

PREPARATION
1. Wash and dry duck.

2. Combine plum sauce, ginger, garlic, brown bean sauce, and 2 tablespoons honey. Spread inside the duck cavity.

3. Combine the remaining 2 tablespoons honey and soy sauce and rub evenly over the skin.

COOKING
1. Preheat a wok, add oil, and heat to 350°F. Roll duck in oil and brown slightly on all sides. Remove duck from oil and place on a heatproof platter.

2. Steam duck for 2 hours over a wok with plenty of water in the bottom. If you don't have a wok or a platter to fit it, use a pan which fits your steamer. Remove and cut into bite-size pieces.

3. Pour the juices from the cooking platter into a saucepan and bring to a boil. Add dissolved cornstarch and stir until the sauce thickens.

4. Add salt to taste. Pour sauce over duck.

STUFFED EIGHT PRECIOUS DUCK WITH PEARLS

Another of Madame Sun's favorite recipes.

1	3-pound duck

STUFFING

3	Tbs. vegetable oil
4	dried black mushrooms, soaked 30 minutes and chopped
½	cup chopped bamboo shoots
2	Chinese sausages, finely chopped, or ½ cup chopped Virginia ham
6	scallions, chopped
2	slices gingerroot, chopped
3	ounces canned lotus seeds
1	tsp. salt
1	Tbs. sherry
1	tsp. sesame oil

½	cup cooked glutinous rice
1	tsp. honey
1	Tbs. light soy sauce
3	cups vegetable oil
1	Tbs. dark soy sauce
2	tsp. cornstarch dissolved in 1½ Tbs. water
24	pearl onions

PREPARATION

1. Clean duck inside and out. Dry.

2. Prepare stuffing: Heat oil in a wok and stir-fry the mushrooms, bamboo shoots, sausages, scallions, ginger, and lotus seeds for 2 to 3 minutes. Add salt, sherry, and sesame oil. Mix well and stir-fry for 2 to 3 minutes. Add rice and cool.

3. Stuff duck and sew vent closed. Press wings down. Brush duck with honey and light soy sauce.

COOKING

1. Preheat a wok and add oil. When hot, deep-fry duck until golden brown on all sides. Remove duck to a

heatproof dish and brush with dark soy sauce.

2. Steam duck for about 2 hours, or until done. Remove and arrange on serving platter. Keep warm.

3. Drain juices from the cooking dish into a saucepan and bring to a boil. Add dissolved cornstarch and cook until thickened. Pour over duck.

4. Boil pearl onions for 5 minutes or until barely tender, and place around duck on platter.

Makes 6 to 8 servings

ALMOND DUCK

1   4- to 5-pound duck
2   pieces star anise
2   scallions, with stems tied in a knot
1   slice gingerroot, crushed
2   Tbs. dark soy sauce
1   tsp. light soy sauce
1   tsp. salt
2   Tbs. cornstarch
2   quarts vegetable oil

SAUCE
½   cup white vinegar
3   Tbs. catsup
2   Tbs. honey
2   Tbs. cornstarch dissolved in 3 Tbs. water

¼   cup crushed toasted almonds

PREPARATION
1. Place duck in a large pot and add water to cover. Add star anise, green scallions, ginger, soy sauces, and salt. Cover and turn to high heat (350°F). Bring to a boil, reduce to medium heat, and cook for 2 hours, or until tender.

2. Remove duck from water and cool. Skin, bone, and shred the meat. (If you enjoy the skin, leave some of it on. It will produce a crisper texture after the meat is deep-fried.)

3. Pack the shredded duck firmly into an 8- or 9-inch-square baking pan to a depth of ¾ inch. Sprinkle generously with cornstarch. Turn the pressed meat cake over and sprinkle the other side.

4. Heat water to boiling in the bottom of a steamer. Place the duck in the top section, cover, and steam for 30 minutes. Remove and cool. Refrigerate overnight.

COOKING
1. Cut the chilled duck cake into 4 pieces and drain on paper towels so that there will be no moisture to splatter.

2. In a deep-fryer heat oil to 350°F. Add the duck squares and deep-fry for 10 minutes.

3. While the duck is deep-frying, prepare the sauce. Mix together the vinegar, catsup, and honey. Pour into a skillet and bring to a boil. Add the dissolved cornstarch and cook until the sauce

thickens to the desired consistency.

4. Remove duck from deep-fryer with a slotted spoon and drain on paper towels. Cut into 1-inch squares and place on a serving platter.

5. Pour the sauce over the duck and sprinkle with the crushed almonds. Serve immediately.

Makes 4 to 6 servings

DUCK WITH GINGER AND BEAN SPROUTS

½   duck (about 1½ pounds)
1   Tbs. light soy sauce
2   tsp. cornstarch
¼   pound young fresh
      gingerroot or pickled
      ginger
1   tsp. salt
1   tsp. sugar

SAUCE
¼   cup chicken broth
1   Tbs. light soy sauce
1   Tbs. sherry
½   tsp. sesame oil
½   tsp. sugar
2   tsp. cornstarch

3   Tbs. vegetable oil
1   clove garlic, crushed
1   pound bean sprouts,
      trimmed

PREPARATION
1. Bone duck and cut into thin strips.

2. Combine soy sauce and cornstarch. Mix well. Marinate duck for 15 minutes.

3. Peel ginger and cut into thin strips. Sprinkle with salt and sugar and let stand 30 minutes. Squeeze out juice before using.

4. Combine sauce ingredients and mix well.

COOKING
1. Preheat a wok and add oil. When hot, add garlic and stir-fry for a few minutes.

2. Add duck meat and stir-fry for 10 minutes.

3. Add ginger and stir-fry for 2 minutes.

4. Add bean sprouts and stir-fry for 2 minutes.

5. Add sauce. Bring to a boil, stirring constantly until sauce thickens. Serve hot.

BRAISED DUCK FEET OR CHICKEN FEET
(Old China Recipe)

When my father-in-law served as Ambassador to the United States, invitations to dine at the Chinese Embassy were held in high regard in Washington, D.C. My mother-in-law was known as an accomplished hostess who set a wonderful table. She took a personal interest in every detail of her parties, planning and shopping for each dinner herself, and soon became a familiar figure at the market, selecting vegetables, fruits, fish, and poultry.

On the first occasion that she requested feet for an Embassy party, the poultryman, who had previously just thrown them away, obligingly presented a huge bag of them to my mother-in-law free of charge. A similar order, however, made several weeks after the party, was accompanied by a bill. The poultryman had had so many calls for feet from guests at her dinner that they had now become much-desired items! My grandchildren and I love to chew on braised chicken feet.

24	duck or chicken feet
3	cups chicken broth
3	cups water
½	cup dark soy sauce
¼	cup light soy sauce
2	Tbs. honey
2	cloves garlic, mashed
1	gingerroot, mashed
3	star anise (optional)

PREPARATION
1. Wash and clean duck or chicken feet. (Make sure that all the nails are removed. Ask your butcher to cut them off, or chop them off yourself.) Drain.

2. Parboil feet for 5 minutes. Drain. Pull off the dark outer skin, or "calluses," from the feet. (Parboiling loosens the skin and makes this step easier.)

COOKING
Combine the remaining ingredients with the cleaned and skinned feet in a large pot. Bring to a boil. Reduce heat and simmer for 2 hours. If not tender enough, simmer an additional 30 minutes.

ENTRÉES

Poultry		(Squab)

ROAST SQUAB

This is one of Madame Sun's recipes.

2	squabs
2	Tbs. dark soy sauce
1	Tbs. sugar
1	tsp. salt
1	tsp. five-spice powder
1	star anise
2	slices gingerroot
2	scallions
1	Tbs. vegetable oil
1	quart vegetable oil for deep-frying
20	raw shrimp chips

PREPARATION

1. Wash and dry squabs.

2. Combine soy sauce, sugar, salt, five spices, and star anise. Rub the squabs inside and outside with this mixture.

3. Stuff each squab with a slice of ginger and a scallion.

4. Grease a roasting pan with 1 tablespoon oil and place the squabs in it.

COOKING

1. Preheat oven to 375°F.

2. Roast squabs for 1 hour.

3. Heat oil and deep-fry shrimp chips until puffy.

4. Cut each squab into 6 to 8 pieces and place on a serving platter.

5. Surround squab with chips. Serve hot.

STRING OF JADE WITH MINCED SQUAB

This dish is served as a first course. Each person takes a lettuce leaf and rolls it up with about 2 tablespoons of the squab mixture. The roll is eaten like a tortilla, with the fingers.

2	squabs or Cornish game hens
¼	cup dried black mushrooms
3	Tbs. vegetable oil
2	slices gingerroot
1	tsp. dark soy sauce
½	tsp. salt
½	tsp. sugar
¼	cup chopped water chestnuts
¼	cup canned diced bamboo shoots
¼	cup chopped cooked Virginia ham
1	tsp. sesame oil
1	cup cooked hot fresh or frozen tiny green peas
8	lettuce leaves

PREPARATION

1. Skin, bone, and mince squabs.

2. Soak mushrooms in warm water for 15 minutes. Drain, cut off tough stems, and chop.

COOKING

1. Preheat wok over high heat and add oil. When hot, swirl ginger around the wok. Remove and discard the ginger.

2. Add chopped squab and stir-fry for 2 to 3 minutes.

3. Add mushrooms and stir-fry for 1 minute.

4. Add soy sauce, salt, and sugar; stir-fry for 1 minute.

5. Stir in water chestnuts, bamboo shoots, and ham. Stir in sesame oil and immediately place mixture on a serving platter.

6. Place peas around the squab mixture for an attractive presentation.

7. Accompany with lettuce leaves on a separate platter.

ENTRÉES

Seafood	魚蝦類	

PEPPER LOBSTER

1	2-pound lobster
1	tsp. garlic salt
½	tsp. sugar
1	Tbs. sherry
2	Tbs. flour

SAUCE

3	Tbs. chicken broth
2	tsp. sherry
1	tsp. light soy sauce
½	tsp. cornstarch

¼	cup vegetable oil
1	slice gingerroot, finely chopped
1	Tbs. ground peppercorns
1	dried chili pepper, ground

PREPARATION

1. Wash and dry lobster. Cut into bite-size pieces.

2. Sprinkle with garlic salt, sugar, and sherry, and dust with flour. Let stand 30 minutes.

3. Combine sauce ingredients.

COOKING

1. Preheat a wok and add oil. When it is hot, add lobster and gently stir-fry for 2 to 3 minutes, or until lobster is just done. Remove with slotted spoon and keep warm.

2. Drain wok, reserving 1 tablespoon oil. Heat and add ginger, peppers, and lobster. Stir-fry for a few seconds. Add sauce and mix well. Serve immediately.

SPICY SHRIMP

12	jumbo shrimp
3	Tbs. vegetable oil
2	cloves garlic, crushed
2	scallions, sliced diagonally
1	slice gingerroot
1	Tbs. hot chili sauce
2	tsp. dark soy sauce
1	tsp. light soy sauce
1	Tbs. red wine
1	tsp. sugar
½	tsp. salt

PREPARATION

Wash shrimp. With knife or pair of scissors, open up the back of each shrimp and pull out the black vein with a toothpick. Remove the sharp point of the tail. Dry shrimp thoroughly on paper towels.

COOKING

1. Preheat a wok or deep skillet and add oil. When hot, add garlic, scallions, ginger, and hot chili sauce. Stir around in wok.

2. Add shrimp one at a time, on the flat side. Quick-fry for 2 minutes, or until pink.

3. Stir in remaining ingredients then remove from heat. Serve hot.

SHRIMP IN GREEN PEPPER

½ pound shrimp
¼ cup finely chopped water chestnuts
2 cloves garlic, finely chopped
1 tsp. light soy sauce
½ tsp. cornstarch
4 medium green peppers

SAUCE
1½ Tbs. vegetable oil
1 Tbs. dark soy sauce
1 tsp. hot sauce
1 tsp. wine vinegar
1 tsp. oyster sauce
½ tsp. honey
1 tsp. cornstarch dissolved in 2 Tbs. water

PREPARATION
1. Clean, shell, and devein shrimp. Finely chop and combine with water chestnuts, garlic, soy sauce, and cornstarch. Mix well.

2. Cut tops from peppers and reserve. Remove seeds and ribs.

3. Fill peppers with shrimp mixture, replace tops, and put in a deep glass heatproof bowl. Cover with plastic wrap.

COOKING
1. Place bowl in a microwave oven and set on high. Cook for 3 to 5 minutes. If you do not cook with a microwave oven, put the filled peppers in a casserole, cover, and cook in your oven for 20 minutes at 350 degrees.

2. Make sauce: Heat oil in a hot wok and add remaining ingredients, except cornstarch. Bring to a boil. Add dissolved cornstarch and stir until the sauce thickens slightly.

3. Pour sauce over green peppers. Serve hot.

SHRIMP WITH PORK BLACK BEAN SAUCE

This sauce is also known as Shrimp Lobster Sauce.

2   Tbs. salted black beans
2   cloves garlic, minced
1   slice gingerroot, minced
2   Tbs. sherry
1   tsp. light soy sauce
1   tsp. sugar
3   Tbs. vegetable oil
¼   pound ground pork
1   cup chicken broth
2   Tbs. cornstarch
     dissolved in 2 Tbs.
     dark soy sauce
1   pound large shrimp,
     shelled and deveined
2   eggs, beaten with 2 Tbs.
     chicken broth
2   scallions, chopped

PREPARATION
1. Mash black beans with garlic and ginger.

2. In another bowl, mix sherry, light soy sauce, and sugar.

COOKING
1. Preheat a wok and add oil. When hot, add black bean mixture and stir-fry for a few seconds.

2. Add pork and stir-fry for 1 minute.

3. Add sherry mixture and stir-fry for 1 minute.

4. Slowly add chicken broth and dissolved cornstarch. Stir constantly for 4 to 5 minutes, or until sauce thickens.

5. Add shrimp and mix well with sauce. Cook for 2 to 3 minutes.

6. Turn off heat and add egg mixture. Allow to set for 20 to 30 seconds. Do not stir.

7. Place shrimp and sauce on serving platter. Garnish with scallions.

DEEP-FRIED SHRIMP-STUFFED BEAN CURD

BATTER

¼   cup flour
2   Tbs. cornstarch
¼   tsp. baking powder
¼   cup water
2   tsp. vegetable oil
1   small egg, beaten

10 medium shrimp
½   tsp. salt
⅛   tsp. white pepper
4   squares bean curd

DIPPING SAUCE
1   Tbs. dark soy sauce
1   tsp. light soy sauce
1   tsp. wine vinegar
½   tsp. sesame oil
½   tsp. hot chili sauce
¼   tsp. sugar
1   Tbs. chopped scallion

1   cup vegetable oil

PREPARATION

1. Combine batter ingredients and stir until smooth. Allow to stand for 1 hour before using.

2. Shell and devein shrimps. Mince and mix with salt and pepper.

3. Wash and drain bean curd. Cut into approximately 1-inch squares and dry in paper towels.

4. Make a small, shallow depression on one side of each bean curd. Stuff with about a teaspoonful of minced shrimp.

5. Combine ingredients for dipping sauce.

COOKING

1. Preheat a wok and add oil.

2. Dip stuffed bean curd into batter and let excess drip off. Slip into oil and deep-fry 3 or 4 at a time until golden brown on all sides. (Use more oil if you wish to fry more squares at one time.)

3. Serve with dipping sauce.

CRAB MEAT WITH STRAW MUSHROOMS

One of Madame Sun's favorite seafood recipes.

SAUCE
½   cup chicken broth
½   tsp. salt (optional)
½   tsp. sugar
½   tsp. cornstarch

1   pound fresh or canned
          straw mushrooms
3   Tbs. vegetable oil
½   cup chicken broth
½   tsp. salt (optional)
4 to 5 ounces fresh or frozen
          crab meat, shredded

PREPARATION
1. Combine sauce ingredients
    and mix well.

2. Wash and drain mushrooms.

COOKING
1. Preheat a wok or deep skillet
    and add 1 tablespoon oil.
    When hot, add mushrooms,
    chicken broth, and salt; stir-
    fry for 1 minute. Discard the
    liquid and place the
    mushrooms in a serving dish.

2. In the same wok, heat 2
    tablespoons oil to boiling.
    Add the crab meat and stir-
    fry for a few seconds.

3. Add sauce and stir-fry until
    the sauce thickens. Pour over
    the mushrooms and serve.

CRAB MEAT WITH ASPARAGUS

SAUCE

2	egg whites
½	tsp. salt (optional)
½	tsp. sugar
½	tsp. cornstarch
½	cup chicken broth

1	pound asparagus
4	Tbs. vegetable oil
2	cloves garlic, crushed
½	tsp. salt (optional)
½	cup chicken broth
4 to 5 ounces fresh or frozen crab meat, shredded	

PREPARATION

1. Prepare sauce: Whip egg whites until stiff. Fold in remaining ingredients.

2. Wash and clean asparagus. Discard tough stems. Slice diagonally into 1½-inch lengths.

COOKING

1. Preheat a wok and add 2 tablespoons oil. When hot, add garlic and stir-fry for a few seconds.

2. Add asparagus, salt, and chicken broth; stir-fry for 2 to 3 minutes. Drain and keep warm on a platter.

3. Heat the remaining 2 tablespoons oil in the wok. Add crab meat and stir-fry for a few seconds.

4. Add sauce, stir-fry for a few seconds, then pour over asparagus. Serve immediately.

STEAMED SCALLOPS WITH GARLIC

1½   pounds scallops

MARINADE
1   slice gingerroot, finely
        chopped
1   Tbs. chopped scallion
1   Tbs. rice wine
dash white pepper

10   cloves garlic
4   Tbs. vegetable oil
2   Tbs. chicken broth
1   tsp. light soy sauce
1   tsp. cornstarch
½   tsp. salt
¼   tsp. sugar
20   cherry tomatoes

PREPARATION
1. Clean scallops.

2. Combine marinade
   ingredients and mix well.
   Marinate scallops for about 5
   minutes.

3. Peel garlic and cut off ends.
   (Garlic soaked in cold water
   several hours becomes easier
   to peel.)

COOKING
1. Preheat a wok or deep skillet
   and add 2 tablespoons oil.
   Drain scallops (reserve
   marinade) and add. Stir-fry
   for 2 to 3 minutes, or until
   scallops turn white. Remove
   scallops and arrange in the
   center of a platter. Keep
   warm.

2. Heat the remaining 2
   tablespoons oil to moderately
   hot. Add garlic and stir-fry
   until light brown.

3. Add chicken broth, cover,
   and simmer for 5 minutes, or
   until hot.

4. Add reserved marinade and
   heat.

5. Add soy sauce, cornstarch,
   salt, and sugar. Bring to a boil
   and stir until the sauce
   thickens.

6. Alternate garlic and tomatoes
   around scallops, pour sauce
   over scallops, and serve
   immediately.

FISH IN BLACK BEAN SAUCE

12   ounces fish fillets
       (preferably sole)

MARINADE
2   slices gingerroot, cut into
      thin strips
2   tsp. sherry
1   tsp. light soy sauce
1   tsp. cornstarch
½   tsp. sugar

4   Tbs. vegetable oil
2   Tbs. black bean sauce
1   scallion, cut into 1-inch
      strips

PREPARATION
1. Cut fish into 2"-×-½" pieces.

2. Combine marinade
ingredients and mix well.
Marinate fish for 30 minutes.

COOKING
1. Preheat a wok and add oil.
When hot, add black bean
sauce and stir-fry for a few
seconds.

2. Add fish and gently stir-fry
for 3 to 4 minutes.

3. Add scallion and remove
from heat. Serve hot.

STEAMED WHOLE FISH

1   1½ - to 2-pound whole
       fish, cleaned
salt
2   scallions, diagonally
       thin-sliced
1   slice gingerroot, peeled
       and cut into thin strips
4   Tbs. vegetable oil
1   Tbs. dark soy sauce
1   tsp. light soy sauce

PREPARATION
1. Scald fish. Slash diagonally 3 times on each side, about ¼ - inch deep.

2. Lightly salt inside and out, and put on a heatproof platter which fits in a steamer.

3. Arrange the scallions and ginger slices in an attractive pattern across the slashes.

COOKING
1. Bring water in the bottom section of a steamer to a boil. Place the platter in the section above the water, cover, and steam for 10 minutes.

2. Just before serving, heat vegetable oil and pour it over the fish, then sprinkle on the soy sauces.

Note: If you do not have a steamer, substitute a roasting pan, placing the platter on a rack. Be sure that the water does not come up to the platter.

FISH SAUTÉED IN CHICKEN BROTH

Part of the Long Life Diet.

½   cup chicken broth
½   tsp. Colman's prepared
     mustard
1   pound rock cod or other
     hard-flesh fish, cut
     into ¼-inch slices
1   scallion, finely chopped
1   tsp. cornstarch dissolved
     in 1 Tbs. water
pepper to taste

COOKING
1. In a wok or deep skillet bring chicken broth to a boil. Add mustard and stir well.

2. Add the fish and scallion. Mix gently.

3. Make a hole in the center of the food by gently moving the fish to the edge of the wok. Add dissolved cornstarch and stir until it thickens.

4. Mix in the fish and add pepper to taste. Serve hot.

FILLET OF FISH IN WINE SAUCE

1   cup dried cloud ears
1   pound sole, grouper, or
       flounder fillets
1   egg white
1   tsp. salt
½   tsp. sugar
1   Tbs. cornstarch

WINE SAUCE
1   cup chicken broth
2   Tbs. white wine
2   tsp. sugar
2   tsp. cornstarch
1   tsp. salt

4   Tbs. vegetable oil
1   scallion, finely chopped
2   slices gingerroot,
       chopped

PREPARATION
1. Soak cloud ears in warm water for 15 minutes. Rinse thoroughly and drain.

2. Slant-cut fish into 3"-X-2" slices.

3. Combine fish with egg white, salt, sugar and cornstarch. Mix gently.

3. Combine wine sauce ingredients and mix well.

COOKING
1. Preheat a wok, add 3 tablespoons oil, and heat to 350°F. Gently stir-fry fish for 1 to 2 minutes, or until flesh turns white. Remove from wok.

2. Heat remaining 1 tablespoon oil. Add scallion, ginger, and cloud ears. Stir-fry for a few seconds.

3. Add wine sauce, stirring constantly until sauce boils and thickens.

4. Return fish to wok. Mix with wine sauce.

5. Place fish in the center of a serving plate and surround with cloud ears. Serve hot.

YELLOW CROAKER WITH PINE NUTS

1   2½- to 3-pound whole
    yellow croaker, red
    cod, or bass, cleaned

MARINADE
2   slices gingerroot, finely
    chopped
1   scallion, finely chopped
2   Tbs. white wine
1   tsp. sesame oil
1   tsp. salt

2   Tbs. cornstarch
3   dried black mushrooms

SAUCE
2   Tbs. water
1   Tbs. white wine
1   Tbs. white vinegar
1   Tbs. dark soy sauce

1   tsp. light soy sauce
1   tsp. sugar
2   Tbs. cornstarch
2   slices gingerroot
1   scallion, chopped

1   quart vegetable oil
¼   cup pine nuts
2   Tbs. diced bamboo
    shoots
1   Tbs. diced Virginia ham
1   Tbs. fresh green peas

PREPARATION
1. Cut off fish head and reserve.
   With a knife, fillet along
   bones on each side to the tail.
   Cut out and discard bones,
   leaving the two fillets
   attached to the tail.

2. Combine marinade
   ingredients and mix well.
   Marinate fish head and fillets
   for 30 minutes. Rub fish with
   cornstarch, lifting by tail to
   shake off any excess.

3. Soak mushrooms in warm
   water for 30 minutes. Discard
   stems and dice.

4. Combine sauce ingredients
   and mix well.

COOKING
1. Preheat a wok and add oil.
   When hot, deep-fry fish head
   and fillets for 4 to 5 minutes,
   or until fish is done. Drain
   and place on a large serving
   platter. Keep warm.

(*continued*)

119

2. Deep-fry pine nuts until golden brown. Drain and set aside.

3. Pour off all but 2 tablespoons oil from wok. Heat and add mushrooms, bamboo shoots, ham, and green peas. Stir-fry for a few seconds.

4. Add sauce and stir until it thickens. Add pine nuts.

5. Mound the ingredients on the fillets between the head and the tail to resemble the shape of a fish. Serve hot.

SWEET AND SOUR WHOLE FISH

A tasty and attractive dish that Madame Sun liked to serve.

1	2- to 3-pound sea bass or red snapper, cleaned
1	tsp. salt
1	egg, beaten
1	cup all-purpose flour

SAUCE

1	cup water
½	cup catsup
2	Tbs. white vinegar
2	Tbs. honey
1	Tbs. vegetable oil
1	cup green pepper chunks
½	cup white onion chunks
½	cup canned pineapple chunks
1	Tbs. cornstarch dissolved in 3 Tbs. water
3	cups vegetable oil

PREPARATION

1. Dry fish and salt inside and out. Make 3 slashes ¼-inch deep on each side.

2. Brush fish with beaten egg, then roll in flour.

COOKING

1. Prepare sauce: In a wok or skillet bring water, catsup, vinegar, honey, and oil to a boil. Add green pepper and onion. Return to a boil and boil for 1 minute. Add pineapple, return to a boil, and stir in the dissolved cornstarch. Stir until thickened. Set aside, keeping warm.

2. Pour enough vegetable oil to a depth of 3 inches in a roasting pan and heat to 375°F.

3. Immerse the head of the fish in the hot oil very gently so that there is no splatter, then slide in the rest of the fish. Deep-fry for 3 to 5 minutes on each side. Remove and drain on paper towels. Place on a platter.

4. Pour the sauce over the fish and serve immediately so that the fish does not become soggy.

LEMON FISH

BATTER
1   cup all-purpose flour
¼   cup cornstarch
½   tsp. baking powder
½   cup water
1   egg, beaten
1   Tbs. vegetable oil

2   quarts vegetable oil
2   ½-pound sole fillets
½   cup lemon juice
2   Tbs. honey
2   tsp. cornstarch dissolved
     in 2 Tbs. water
parsley sprigs
1   lemon, sliced and cut
     into halves

PREPARATION
Combine batter ingredients and stir until well blended.

COOKING
1. Preheat a wok, add oil, and heat to 350°F.

2. Drop the sole into the batter and cover completely. Lift out gently and let excess batter drip off. Slip into the hot oil and deep-fry for 2 minutes, until light golden brown. Remove and drain on paper towels.

3. In a small saucepan combine the lemon juice, honey, and dissolved cornstarch. Bring to a boil and pour over the fish.

4. Garnish with parsley and lemon slices arranged alternately around fish on platter. Serve immediately.

SQUID IN GARLIC AND BLACK BEAN SAUCE

1   pound squid
3   Tbs. vegetable oil
1   Tbs. black bean sauce
1   clove garlic, minced
2   slices gingerroot
1   small green pepper, cut
       into chunks
¼   cup sliced white onion
¼   cup chicken broth
1   Tbs. red wine
1   tsp. light soy sauce
1   tsp. cornstarch dissolved
       in 2 tsp. water

PREPARATION

Clean squid. Remove outer layer of skin and drain. Cut into bite-size pieces.

COOKING

1. Preheat a wok and add oil. When very hot, add black bean sauce, garlic, and 1 slice of the ginger. Stir-fry for a few seconds.

2. Add squid and stir-fry for 2 to 3 minutes, until they curl up and are just done. Remove from wok and set aside.

3. Add green pepper and onion; stir-fry for 1 minute.

4. Add chicken broth, wine, soy sauce, and remaining slice of ginger; stir-fry for 1 minute.

5. Return squid and stir.

6. Add dissolved cornstarch and stir for a few seconds. Serve hot.

FROG LEGS AND BITTER MELON IN BLACK BEAN SAUCE

1	pound frozen frog legs, thawed
5	slices gingerroot, crushed
1	tsp. sugar
1	tsp. cornstarch
¼	tsp. salt
⅛	tsp. white pepper
2	10-ounce bitter melons

SAUCE

2	Tbs. water
1	Tbs. sherry
1	tsp. oyster sauce
1	tsp. sesame oil
1	tsp. sugar
1	tsp. cornstarch

3	Tbs. vegetable oil
1	Tbs. black bean sauce
1	clove garlic, crushed
1	tsp. light soy sauce

PREPARATION

1. Dry frog legs and cut into bite-size pieces.

2. Add half of the gingerroot, and the sugar, cornstarch, salt, and pepper. Mix well and marinate for 20 minutes.

3. Cut the bitter melons in half lengthwise. Scoop out seeds and spongy parts and discard. Cut into medium pieces. Parboil in a pot for about 5 minutes (longer if you prefer a mild-tasting melon). Drain, rinse in cold water, and set aside.

4. Combine sauce ingredients and mix well.

COOKING

1. Preheat a wok and add oil. When hot, pour in black bean sauce, add garlic, soy sauce, and remaining ginger.

2. Add frog legs and stir-fry for about 10 minutes, or until done. Do not overcook or they will become tough.

3. Add bitter melon and stir gently for about 3 minutes.

4. Make a hole in the center of the mixture and add sauce. Stir until it thickens. Mix in frog legs and bitter melon.

Note: If you bone the frog legs, they may be easier to serve.

VEGETABLES

蔬菜類

CHINESE EGGPLANT SALAD

3	½-pound Chinese eggplants
2	Tbs. vinegar
1	Tbs. light soy sauce
1	Tbs. sesame oil
1	tsp. hot chili paste
¼	tsp. salt
1	slice gingerroot, finely chopped
1	clove garlic, finely chopped
1	scallion, finely chopped

PREPARATION

1. Wash and peel eggplants. Cut off and discard ends.

2. Combine vinegar, soy sauce, sesame oil, chili paste, and salt.

COOKING

1. In a pot of salted boiling water cook eggplants gently for 10 to 15 minutes, or until tender.

2. Place eggplants under cold running water for 1 minute; drain. Shred loosely lengthwise.

3. Blend soy sauce mixture with ginger and garlic and pour over eggplant.

4. Sprinkle with chopped scallion and serve.

FIVE-SPICE EGGPLANT

3	Tbs. vegetable oil
1	clove garlic, crushed
1	scallion with 6 inches of stem, cut diagonally into 2-inch pieces
4	Chinese eggplants, each cut into 6 wedges
¼	cup chicken broth
1	Tbs. red wine vinegar
1	Tbs. chili paste
1	Tbs. dark soy sauce
1	tsp. light soy sauce

COOKING

1. Preheat wok to hot (350°F). Add oil, garlic, and scallion. Stir-fry a second.

2. Add eggplant and stir-fry for a few seconds.

3. Add chicken broth, cover, and cook 2 minutes.

4. Add vinegar, chili paste, and soy sauces; stir-fry for a few seconds. Serve hot.

SPINACH AND BAMBOO SHOOTS

This recipe is part of the Long Life Diet. It is important to use homemade chicken broth, as it can be unsalted, whereas canned broth will be heavily salted.

½   **cup chicken broth**
2   **bunches spinach, inner leaves only, cleaned**
1   **cup canned sliced bamboo shoots, rinsed and drained**
1   **Tbs. lemon juice**
1   **Tbs. chopped scallion**
1   **tsp. hot mustard**

COOKING
1. Preheat a wok or deep skillet. Add chicken broth and bring to a boil.

2. Add spinach and stir until leaves turn soft, about 1 minute.

3. Add bamboo shoots and stir for 1 minute.

4. Add lemon juice, scallion, and hot mustard. Stir and drain. Serve hot.

VEGETARIAN'S DELIGHT

It is well-recognized that Chinese vegetables, with their high fiber content, are cleansing to the system.

2	ounces cellophane noodles (bean threads)
5	dried black mushrooms
¾	cup chicken broth
1	cup sliced Chinese celery cabbage
½	cup sliced bamboo shoots
½	cup sliced water chestnuts
½	cup sliced snow peas
1	Tbs. dark soy sauce
2	tsp. light soy sauce

PREPARATION
In separate bowls soak noodles and mushrooms in hot water for 30 minutes. Drain. Slice mushrooms.

COOKING
1. In a preheated wok bring chicken broth to a boil.

2. Add celery cabbage and cook for 3 to 5 minutes, or until just soft.

3. Add noodles, mushrooms, bamboo shoots, water chestnuts, and snow peas; stir well.

4. Add soy sauces and mix well. Cook gently until done, 4 to 5 minutes.

Note: If the dish appears too dry, add a little more chicken broth or water. Use nonsalt soy sauce for a strict diet.

Makes 4 to 6 servings

BROCCOLI WITH BUTTON MUSHROOMS

If one is on a special diet, eliminate the oil, salt, and sugar and use chicken broth for cooking.

1	pound broccoli
3	Tbs. vegetable oil
1	slice gingerroot
½	tsp. salt
½	tsp. sugar
1	8-ounce can whole button mushrooms, drained
½	cup chicken broth

PREPARATION
Wash and drain broccoli. Discard tough or wilted outer leaves. Cut off and discard tough base end. Scrape away tough fibers from floret stems and cut into 3-inch pieces.

COOKING
1. Preheat a wok and add oil. When hot, add ginger and stir-fry for a few seconds.

2. Add broccoli, salt, and sugar; stir-fry for a few seconds.

3. Add mushrooms and chicken broth and stir-fry for a few seconds. Cover and cook for 1 to 2 minutes, or until broccoli is tender and green. Serve hot.

CHINESE VEGETABLE CHOP SUEY

Chop suey is probably one of the most popular of all Chinese dishes in America, yet if all the stories about this tasty concoction's origin are true, it did not originate in China. How then did it really come into being?

In the Wu family there is a story that has been told now for several generations and all members of our family vow it is true! It stems from my husband's grandfather, the legendary Dr. Wu T'ing-fang, first Chinese Ambassador to the United States and renowned diplomat.

Once, when he was entertaining at a dinner party at the Chinese Embassy in Washington, he had his chef prepare a dish of tasty sliced ingredients. His guests liked this particular dish so much, they all asked what it was called. But, since there was no generally accepted name for it, Dr. Wu explained that he called it "chop suey" because it was made up of sliced items mixed together and served hot.

In the Chinese language, chop means "sliced" and suey means "small pieces or slices."

The word quickly spread, as Dr. Wu was a very well-known host, and people began asking for chop suey in restaurants. It wasn't long before many chefs learned how to make it, and chop suey became a popular, much-desired entrée to Americans seeking Chinese food.

And that is the way it is told in the Wu family!

4	**Tbs. vegetable oil**
1	**slice gingerroot**
1	**clove garlic, crushed**
2	**cups thin-sliced Chinese celery cabbage**
1	**tsp. salt**
½	**tsp. sugar**
¼	**cup chicken broth**
½	**cup Chinese pea pods**
½	**cup thin-sliced bamboo shoots**
½	**cup thin-sliced mushrooms**

COOKING

1. Preheat a wok and swirl around oil. Rub ginger and garlic on wok and discard.

2. Add cabbage and stir.

3. Add salt, sugar, and chicken broth. Stir, cover, and cook for 3 minutes.

4. Add remaining ingredients and stir for 1 minute. Serve hot.

STIR-FRIED GREEN PEPPERS AND LETTUCE

A Long Life Diet recipe.

1	head iceberg lettuce
2	medium leeks
2	medium green peppers
1	celery heart
1	tsp. cornstarch dissolved in 1 Tbs. water
1	tsp. hot mustard
½	cup chicken broth
1	Tbs. lemon juice

PREPARATION

1. Diagonally slice lettuce into 3-inch-long pieces.

2. Diagonally thin-slice leek into 3-inch-long pieces.

3. Remove seeds from green pepper and thin-slice into 2½"-×-⅛" pieces.

4. Thin-slice celery into 2-inch pieces.

5. Mix cornstarch and hot mustard until smooth. Set aside.

COOKING

1. Preheat a wok or deep skillet and add chicken broth. When it comes to a rolling boil, add celery and green peppers. Reduce heat to medium and cook for 1 minute.

2. Add lettuce and leeks; stir for a few seconds.

3. Add cornstarch mixture and lemon juice. Stir until cornstarch thickens. Serve hot.

LEEK WITH STRING BEANS AND CARROTS

For the Long Life Diet, eliminate the oil, sugar, and salt, and cook vegetables completely in chicken broth.

3	Tbs. vegetable oil
1	clove garlic, crushed
½	pound string beans, cut into 2-inch lengths
2	carrots, thin-sliced
½	cup thin-sliced leek
¼	cup chicken broth
½	tsp. sugar
¼	tsp. salt

COOKING

1. Preheat a wok and add oil. When hot, add garlic, and stir for a few seconds, then discard.

2. Add string beans and carrots; stir-fry for 1 minute.

3. Add leek, chicken broth, sugar, and salt. Stir-fry for 1 to 2 minutes.

4. Remove to platter and serve immediately.

BEAN SPROUT AND CUCUMBER SALAD

Just as the Chinese hot pot is a wonderful dish for cold weather, this salad is ideal for a hot summer night. Not only is it cool and refreshing, but it uses simple ingredients that require no cooking over a hot stove.

2	cucumbers
2	cups trimmed bean sprouts
2	Tbs. red wine vinegar
1	Tbs. sesame oil
1	Tbs. dark soy sauce
1	tsp. light soy sauce
1	tsp. honey

PREPARATION

1. Peel cucumbers and cut in half lengthwise. Scoop out seeds and cut cucumber into thin slices.

2. In boiling water sufficient to cover, add the cucumbers and bean sprouts. Turn off heat immediately and stir for a few seconds.

3. Drain in a colander and rinse under running cold water a few minutes. Drain well. Chill until serving time.

COOKING

When ready to serve, put chilled bean sprouts and cucumbers in a salad bowl and mix with the remaining ingredients. Serve immediately.

JELLYFISH AND CUCUMBER SALAD

2	cups shredded dried jellyfish
2	cucumbers
3	Tbs. red wine vinegar
1	Tbs. sesame oil
1	Tbs. dark soy sauce
1	tsp. light soy sauce
1	tsp. honey

PREPARATION
1. Soak jellyfish in warm (not hot) water overnight. Drain carefully and rinse off salt.

2. Peel and cut the cucumbers in half lengthwise. Scoop out the seeds and cut cucumber into thin slices.

COOKING
1. In a salad bowl combine the remaining ingredients. Add jellyfish and cucumbers and mix well.

2. Chill several hours before serving.

ZUCCHINI WITH MUSHROOMS

Using chicken broth rather than oil, this recipe was developed for the Long Life Diet.

½   cup chicken broth
3   cups ½-inch slices
        zucchini
3   cloves garlic, minced
1   Tbs. hot mustard
2   cups whole mushrooms,
        soaked 15 minutes
1   medium green pepper,
        cut into ½-inch strips
1   Tbs. chopped scallion
½   tsp. white pepper

COOKING
1. Preheat a wok or deep skillet and add chicken broth. Bring to a boil. Add zucchini, garlic, and hot mustard. Stir briefly.

2. Add mushrooms and green pepper and stir for 1 minute. Reduce heat to medium and cook for 2 minutes.

3. Add scallion and white pepper. Increase heat to high and stir for a few seconds. Serve hot.

ASPARAGUS WITH BLACK BEAN SAUCE

3	Tbs. vegetable oil
2	cloves garlic, crushed
1	Tbs. black bean sauce
2	cups asparagus pieces (tips and tender stalks), cut diagonally into 1½-inch lengths
3	Tbs. water
1	Tbs. dark soy sauce
½	tsp. sugar

COOKING

1. Preheat a wok and add oil. When hot, add crushed garlic and black bean sauce. Stir-fry for a few seconds.

2. Add asparagus and stir-fry for 1 minute.

3. Add water, soy sauce, and sugar. Cover and cook for 2 minutes, then remove cover and stir-fry for 1 minute. Serve hot.

HOT AND SOUR RED CABBAGE

1	medium-size head red cabbage
3	Tbs. vegetable oil
2	cloves garlic, crushed
2	slices gingerroot
¼	cup chicken broth
2	Tbs. red wine vinegar
1	Tbs. dark soy sauce
1	tsp. light soy sauce
1	tsp. honey
2	dried red chili peppers
1	scallion, chopped

PREPARATION
Wash cabbage and cut into quarters. Cut away core, then cut each quarter horizontally into halves.

COOKING
1. Preheat a wok and add oil. When hot, add garlic and ginger and stir-fry for a few seconds.

2. Add cabbage and stir-fry for 1 minute.

3. Add chicken broth, cover, and cook for 1 minute.

4. Add vinegar, soy sauces, honey and peppers and stir-fry for 1 minute.

5. Sprinkle with scallions. Serve hot.

WATERCRESS WITH BAMBOO SHOOTS

3	Tbs. vegetable oil
1	slice gingerroot, sliced thin
1	bunch watercress, stems removed
1	tsp. salt
½	tsp. sugar
1	Tbs. water
1	tsp. light soy sauce
1	cup sliced bamboo shoots, rinsed

COOKING

1. Preheat a wok and swirl with oil. Stir-fry ginger for 1 to 2 seconds, then discard.

2. Add watercress and stir-fry for 3 to 4 minutes.

3. Add salt, sugar, water, and soy sauce; stir-fry for 1 minute.

4. Add bamboo shoots and stir-fry for 1 minute. Serve hot.

FOUR-VEGETABLE DELIGHT

For Long Life Diet, omit salt, sugar, and oil and cook vegetables in chicken broth.

3	Tbs. vegetable oil
1	slice gingerroot, chopped
18	small Chinese white cabbage hearts
¼	cup chicken broth
1	tsp. salt
½	tsp. sugar
2	6-ounce cans button mushrooms, drained and rinsed
12	cherry tomatoes
18	canned baby corn on cob, rinsed
1	Tbs. cornstarch dissolved in 2 Tbs. water

COOKING

1. Preheat a wok or deep skillet, add oil, and heat to 350°F. Add ginger.

2. Stir-fry cabbage hearts for 1 minute.

3. Add chicken broth, salt, and sugar. Cover and cook for 2 minutes.

4. Add mushrooms, tomatoes, and baby corn; stir-fry for 1 minute.

5. Add dissolved cornstarch and stir-fry for a few seconds, until thickened. Serve hot.

TO SERVE

1. For an attractive platter, arrange the vegetables in a repeating pattern of 6 cabbage hearts and 6 baby corns around the rim of the platter.

2. Place the mushrooms in the center and surround them with a ring of cherry tomatoes. The platter will resemble a colorful flower in full bloom.

Makes 6 servings

CARROTS, CAULIFLOWER, AND BRUSSELS SPROUTS

This is a Long Life Diet recipe. Add salt and sugar to taste if you are not following a restricted diet.

½   pound cauliflower florets
¼   pound carrots
¼   pound Brussels sprouts
½   cup chicken broth
1   slice gingerroot
1   Tbs. hot mustard
¼   cup scallions

PREPARATION
1. Clean and cut cauliflower florets into 2-inch pieces.

2. Clean and scrape carrots. Thin-slice diagonally into ¼"-×-1½" pieces.

3. Clean Brussels sprouts and halve.

COOKING
1. Preheat a wok and add chicken broth. Bring to a boil and add ginger and hot mustard.

3. Add cauliflower, carrots, and Brussels sprouts. Cover and cook for 3 minutes.

4. Add scallions and stir. Serve hot.

QUICK-FRIED ROMAINE LETTUCE

1	head romaine lettuce
3	Tbs. vegetable oil
2	scallions, thin-sliced
1	slice gingerroot, crushed
¼	cup chicken broth
1	tsp. sugar
1	tsp. soy sauce

PREPARATION
Clean lettuce thoroughly and discard tough leaves. Separate leaves and cut them into 3-inch lengths. Cut heart lengthwise into 2 or 3 pieces.

COOKING
1. Preheat a wok and add oil. When hot, add scallions and ginger; stir-fry lightly.

2. Add lettuce and stir-fry for 1 minute.

3. Add chicken broth, sugar, and soy sauce; stir-fry for 1 minute.

4. Remove lettuce from wok with a slotted spoon. Serve hot.

SWEET AND SOUR CABBAGE SALAD

1½	pounds Chinese white cabbage
1	Tbs. salt
2	hot red peppers, seeded and shredded
1	Tbs. shredded gingerroot
½	cup white vinegar
½	cup water
⅓	cup sugar
1	tsp. peppercorns
1	Tbs. sesame oil

PREPARATION

1. Clean cabbage and cut into 1½-inch shreds. Place in a bowl and sprinkle with salt. Mix well and let stand 4 hours.

2. Squeeze out briny juice and discard. Add hot peppers and ginger. Mix well.

COOKING

1. Preheat a wok or deep skillet. Add vinegar, water, and sugar and bring to a boil.

2. Add peppercorns and sesame oil. Immediately pour over cabbage and mix well.

3. Cool, cover, and refrigerate. The salad will keep for over a week.

Note: Depending on how hot the dried chili peppers you select are, this dish (used almost like a condiment in China) will be just plain hot, or will set your mouth aflame. Chinese eat the cabbage and leave the pepper shreds on the plate.

STIR-FRIED GREEN BEANS WITH CARROTS

½	pound green beans
¼	pound carrots
3	Tbs. vegetable oil
2	cloves garlic, crushed
1	slice gingerroot, crushed
¼	cup chicken broth
1	tsp. honey
1	tsp. dry sherry
1	Tbs. soy sauce

PREPARATION

1. Clean beans and trim. Thin-slice beans lengthwise into 2-inch pieces.

2. Clean and scrape carrots. Cut into 2-inch pieces, then thin-slice lengthwise into same size as green beans.

COOKING

1. Preheat a wok or deep skillet and add oil. When hot, add garlic and ginger; stir-fry for a second and discard.

2. Add beans and carrots and stir-fry for a few seconds.

3. Add chicken broth and stir for 1 minute. Cover and cook 2 minutes over medium heat.

4. Add remaining ingredients and stir for 1 minute. Serve hot.

RICE AND NOODLE DISHES

飯
麵
類

A SHORT STORY ABOUT RICE

For this section on rice and noodles, I would like to stress the importance of rice in the Chinese diet. Cooked in many ways, it is the staple food in China and is eaten very much the way that bread and potatoes are eaten in the West, except that meat, poultry, seafood, and vegetable dishes accompany the rice, instead of the other way around. Rice is also the source of a wine that plays a large part in the preparation of Chinese food and accompanies the food on special occasions. Rice wine was discovered quite by accident and no one at the time realized that it would grow into a nationally popular beverage for all festive meals.

The story goes that it was a busy and forgetful Imperial Chef at the Emperor's Palace who put some rice in an old earthenware jug to soak and unwittingly left it there for several weeks. When he eventually looked into the jug, he was unprepared for what was inside. The unusual bouquet attracted him enough to taste it. His first taste pleased him so much, that he could not stop himself from drinking more. He soon became very happy and started singing at the top of his voice. The Emperor, wondering at this feeling of well-being brought on so rapidly by the liquid, ordered some of the brew for the very special feast he was then serving. During the course of the evening, he realized happily that, one by one, his opponents had become rather jolly and agreeable, thanks to this wonderful drink. Indeed, this was a very valuable thing!

The next morning, however, the Emperor found another side to it, as his own officials were unfit for work, moaning and holding their heads. So he issued a decree on drinking: no drinking on an empty stomach; serve wine only in very small cups; eat while drinking; engage in some mental and physical activity while dining. It worked. The Chinese are really very moderate in their drinking. Intoxication is not common. Wine is always served during meals to create an atmosphere of gaiety and friendship.

FLUFFY BOILED RICE

Electric rice cookers are excellent for preparing rice and do the cooking automatically. Cooked rice to be used in fried rice recipes is best when kept overnight in the refrigerator first. Freshly boiled rice is sticky and will not separate properly for stir-frying.

2   **cups long-grain white or brown rice**
2   **cups water**

COOKING
Wash rice, drain, and put into a 2-quart pot. Add water and cover and stir just enough to keep the rice from sticking to the sides and bottom. Continue cooking, uncovered, over high heat until the water has almost all boiled away. Now cover the pot and turn the burner down to a very low heat, letting the rice simmer for about 15 to 20 minutes.

SUBGUM FRIED RICE

3	Tbs. vegetable oil
2	scallions, finely chopped
2	eggs, well beaten
¼	cup thawed frozen green peas
¼	cup cooked baby shrimp
¼	cup diced cooked ham
3	cups cold cooked rice
1	Tbs. dark soy sauce
1	tsp. light soy sauce

COOKING

1. Preheat a wok and add oil over high heat.

2. Add scallions and eggs and quick-fry.

3. Add peas and shrimp and stir-fry for 1 minute.

4. Add ham and stir-fry for a few seconds.

5. Add rice and soy sauces. Mix thoroughly and stir-fry for 1 minute. Serve hot.

FRIED RICE WITH CHINESE PORK SAUSAGE

3	Tbs. vegetable oil
4	Chinese sausages, diced, or ½ cup diced cooked Virginia ham
2	eggs, well beaten
2	scallions, finely chopped
4	cups cold cooked rice
1	Tbs. dark soy sauce
1	tsp. light soy sauce

COOKING

1. Preheat a wok and add oil over high heat. Add sausage or ham, reduce heat, and cook until brown, 1 to 2 minutes.

2. Add eggs and scallion; stir well.

3. Add rice and soy sauces; stir-fry for 2 to 3 minutes. Serve hot.

FRIED RICE WITH EGGS

Actor Pat O'Brien, an early guest in my restaurant, always ordered "burnt rice," much to the consternation of the chef, who refused to burn it. The impasse was solved when I suggested to the chef that he simply add two more tablespoons of dark soy sauce to the recipe. It was solved, that is, until I related the story in my first book, Madame Wu's Art of Chinese Cooking, *and Pat read it. Now he insists on going into the kitchen to see that the chef almost burns the rice, not merely adds soy sauce as we had done previously.*

3	Tbs. vegetable oil
3	eggs, well beaten
2	scallions, finely chopped
3	cups cold cooked rice
1	Tbs. dark soy sauce
1	tsp. light soy sauce

COOKING

1. Preheat a wok and add oil over high heat. Add eggs and scallions and stir-fry quickly.

2. Add rice and stir-fry for 2 minutes.

3. Add soy sauces and stir-fry for a few seconds, mixing thoroughly. Serve hot.

BEEF FRIED RICE WITH SALT FISH

¼   **pound salt fish**

MARINADE
1   **Tbs. dark soy sauce**
1   **Tbs. sherry**
1   **tsp. cornstarch**
½   **tsp. sugar**

¼   **pound ground round**
        steak
3   **Tbs. vegetable oil**
2   **eggs, well beaten**
3   **cups cold cooked rice**
1   **scallion, finely chopped**

PREPARATION
1. Steam salt fish for 20 minutes. Remove all bones. Dice fish into small pieces.

2. Combine marinade ingredients.

3. Combine ground beef with marinade and mix well. Marinate for at least 30 minutes.

COOKING
1. Preheat a wok and add oil. When hot, add salt fish and stir-fry for a few seconds. (It will give out a strong aroma.)

2. Add marinated beef and stir-fry for 2 to 3 minutes.

3. Add eggs and stir-fry for a few seconds.

4. Add rice and mix in; cook several minutes.

5. Garnish with scallion. Serve hot.

Note: If you like your fried rice moist, add ¼ cup chicken broth to the wok after you add the rice and stir thoroughly for a few seconds.

BEEF CONGEE

MARINADE

2   slices gingerroot,
         crushed
1   Tbs. light soy sauce
¼   tsp. sesame oil
1   tsp. cornstarch
dash white pepper

½   cup ground round beef
½   cup uncooked rice
10   cups chicken broth
 2   scallions, chopped
sesame oil
6–8 eggs

PREPARATION

1. Combine marinade
   ingredients.

2. Combine beef with marinade
   and mix well. Marinate for 15
   to 20 minutes.

COOKING

1. In a large pot, bring rice and
   chicken broth to a boil.
   Reduce heat, cover, and
   simmer 2 hours. (Add boiling
   water if necessary to keep the
   congee from becoming too
   thick.)

2. Add marinated beef. Stir only
   once or twice.

TO SERVE

1. Put ¼ teaspoon chopped
   scallion and a few drops of
   sesame oil in the bottom of
   individual soup bowls. Ladle
   the hot congee into each
   bowl.

2. Thoroughly stir an egg into
   each serving. Eat
   immediately.

Makes 6 to 8 servings.

LEFTOVER CHICKEN WITH NOODLES—SHANGHAI STYLE

1 pound Chinese egg
   noodles, thin noodles,
   or spaghetti
2 quarts boiling water
4 Tbs. vegetable oil
2 Tbs. dark soy sauce
1 cup thin-sliced cooked
   chicken breast
½ cup diagonal-sliced
   scallions, with stems
¼ cup thin-sliced hot green
   pepper, seeded
1 Tbs. cornstarch
   dissolved in 2 Tbs.
   water
1 tsp. light soy sauce

COOKING
1. Cook noodles in boiling
   water until soft, about 10 to
   15 minutes. Drain into a
   colander and rinse under cold
   water for about 2 minutes.
   Drain thoroughly.

2. Preheat a wok over high heat
   and add 2 tablespoons oil.
   When hot, add noodles. Stir-
   fry for 1 minute.

3. Add 1 tablespoon dark soy
   sauce and stir-fry for 1
   minute. Remove to a serving
   platter.

4. Wash, dry, and reheat the
   wok. Heat 2 tablespoons
   vegetable oil. Add chicken
   and stir-fry for 2 minutes.

5. Add scallions and hot pepper;
   stir-fry for 1 minute.

6. Combine dissolved
   cornstarch with soy sauces.
   Stir into chicken mixture.

7. Spoon sauce immediately
   onto noodles. Serve hot.

EGGS

蚤類

HAPPY RED EGGS

Eggs are a symbol of fertility in China, and red is considered a lucky color. Whenever there is a birth in the family, the proud father presents his friends with one of these hard-boiled red eggs instead of a cigar.

12	eggs
1	cup boiling water
30	drops red food coloring (or red Easter egg dye)
1	tsp. vinegar

COOKING

1. Place eggs in a 2-quart pot, cover with water, and bring to a boil over medium heat. Reduce heat and simmer for 10 to 15 minutes. Remove eggs from pot and dry on paper towels.

2. Pour 1 cup boiling water into a bowl deep enough to submerge 1 egg at a time.

3. Add food coloring and vinegar. Dye each egg until it is pinkish-red.

STEAMED EGGS WITH MINCED BEEF

4	eggs, well beaten
2	cups chicken broth
¼	cup minced or ground beef
½	tsp. salt
½	tsp. sugar (optional)
¼	cup minced water chestnuts
1	scallion, finely chopped
1	Tbs. light soy sauce
1	tsp. sesame oil

PREPARATION
Combine eggs, chicken broth, beef, salt, sugar, water chestnuts, and scallion.

COOKING
To steam: Pour egg mixture into a deep heatproof dish and place in a steamer containing 2 inches boiling water. Cover and cook over high heat for 10 minutes. Pour soy sauce and sesame oil over the steamed eggs. Serve hot.

For microwave: Pour egg mixture into a nonmetal heat-proof dish, cover with plastic wrap, and place in oven. Turn dial to high and cook for 6 minutes. Then pour soy sauce and sesame oil over the steamed eggs. Serve hot.

EGGS WITH HAM AND TOMATO

6	eggs
1	tsp. salt
¼	tsp. white pepper
2	medium tomatoes
3	Tbs. vegetable oil
½	cup diced cooked ham
1	sprig Chinese parsley

PREPARATION
1. In a bowl beat eggs. Add salt and pepper and beat again.

2. Scald tomatoes in boiling water for 2 to 3 minutes, then peel, quarter, and remove seeds. Cut into thin slices.

COOKING
1. Preheat a wok and add oil. When hot, stir-fry tomatoes until almost dry.

2. Add ham and stir-fry for a few seconds.

3. Pour in eggs and stir-fry until barely cooked.

4. Garnish with Chinese parsley and serve hot.

PLAIN STEAMED EGGS

This is a delicious main course for a light lunch.

6   **eggs, well beaten**
2   **cups chicken broth**
1   **scallion, white part only, chopped**
1   **tsp. light soy sauce**
1   **tsp. sesame oil**

PREPARATION
1. Beat eggs and chicken broth together.

2. Add scallion and mix well.

COOKING
For microwave: Put egg mixture in a shallow nonmetal heatproof serving bowl. Cover with plastic wrap and place in the oven. Turn dial to high and cook for 6 minutes. Pour soy sauce and sesame oil over the eggs. Serve hot.

To steam: Bring water to a boil in the bottom of a steamer, put bowl in the top section, and reduce heat to medium. Cover and steam for 10 to 15 minutes, or until eggs are set and in custard form. Pour soy sauce and sesame oil over the eggs. Serve hot.

EGGS WITH PORK AND GREEN PEAS

6	eggs
¼	tsp. salt
dash	white pepper
3	Tbs. vegetable oil
½	pound minced or ground pork
¼	cup canned mushrooms
2	tsp. light soy sauce
¼	cup fresh or frozen green peas
2	scallions, finely chopped

PREPARATION

Beat eggs. Season with salt and pepper. Beat again.

COOKING

1. Preheat a wok and add oil. When hot, add pork and stir-fry for 2 minutes.

2. Add mushrooms and soy sauce; stir-fry for a few seconds.

3. Add green peas and stir-fry for a few seconds.

4. Add eggs and stir-fry until eggs are done to your liking.

5. Add scallions and serve immediately.

DESSERTS

甜點心類

MANGO TAPIOCA PUDDING

1	Tbs. agar-agar
½	cup tapioca
8	cups water
½	cup sugar
½	cup milk
2	mangoes or other fresh fruit, cut into ½-inch cubes

PREPARATION
Soak agar-agar in water for 30 minutes.

COOKING
1. In a pot, slowly add tapioca to 2 cups boiling water, stirring constantly. Cook for 5 to 6 minutes over moderate heat. Remove from heat, drain, and add cold water to cool. Drain again.

2. Drain agar-agar and put into pot of 6 cups boiling water. Boil until agar-agar is dissolved.

3. Remove from heat and add sugar, stirring until dissolved.

4. Add milk and mangoes. Add tapioca and pour into mold of desired shape.

5. Cool and refrigerate until firm. Tapioca will sink to the bottom and create a layered effect. Serve chilled.

SWEET RICE PUDDING

2 cups glutinous rice
2 Tbs. vegetable oil
3 Tbs. sugar
3 dates, pitted
2 Tbs. shredded candied
    green papaya
2 Tbs. shredded candied
    red papaya
12 lotus seeds or lichee nuts
3 Tbs. raisins
⅓ cup mashed red beans
⅓ cup candied red beans

SAUCE
1 cup water
3 Tbs. sugar
2 tsp. cornstarch dissolved
    in 2 tsp. water

PREPARATION
1. Soak rice in water for 12 hours. Drain and cook in enough water to cover for 30 minutes. Stir in 1 tablespoon oil and the sugar.

2. Coat a medium-size heatproof bowl with 1 tablespoon oil. Place dates in a cluster in the center of the bowl and arrange the green and red papaya shreds alternately around them.

3. Ring the papaya shreds with lotus seeds and make a final ring with the raisins.

4. Cover the fruit with half the rice and pack down evenly with a spoon.

5. Tamp the mashed red beans down over the rice, and then pack in the remaining rice. Insert the candied red beans around the edge of the bowl.

COOKING
1. Steam for 1 hour. Unmold pudding on a platter.

2. Prepare sauce: Bring water and sugar to a boil. Stir in the dissolved cornstarch and pour the sauce over the pudding. Serve hot.

CANDIED BANANA FRITTERS

4   bananas
1   cup flour
2   eggs, beaten
5   cups vegetable oil for
        deep-frying
2   Tbs. vegetable oil
1   cup water
6   Tbs. sugar
½   tsp. sesame oil
ice water for dipping

PREPARATION
1. Peel bananas and cut into
   bite-size pieces.

2. Coat with flour, dip into
   beaten eggs, then into flour
   again.

COOKING
1. Preheat a wok or deep skillet
   and add oil. When hot, deep-
   fry banana pieces until
   golden brown. Remove and
   keep warm.

2. In a saucepan, heat 2
   tablespoons oil. Add water
   and sugar and stir over
   medium heat until sugar
   melts. Reduce heat and
   simmer, stirring constantly
   until caramel colored.

3. Add sesame oil and mix well.

4. Place the deep-fried bananas
   on a serving platter and pour
   caramel over them evenly.

TO SERVE
Diners dip the banana pieces
into a bowl of ice cold water.
The caramel on the banana
crystallizes, making a cold
crackling exterior, while the
interior is moist and warm.

ALMOND GELATIN AND MIXED FRUITS

½	ounce dried agar-agar, rinsed and drained
5	cups water
½	cup rock sugar or granulated sugar
½	cup milk
1	Tbs. almond extract
1	8-ounce can mixed fruit in syrup

COOKING

1. In a pot, add agar-agar to water and bring to a boil. Boil gently for 30 minutes, or until agar-agar is dissolved.

2. Add sugar, milk, and almond extract. Remove from heat and stir thoroughly. Pour into a flat pan and refrigerate until jelled.

3. Add almond extract to fruit.

4. Cut gelatin into small pieces and place in a serving bowl. Add fruit with syrup. Serve chilled.

Note: If you wish to substitute fresh fruit, omit the 1 tablespoon almond extract and the canned fruit. Make a syrup by boiling 6 cups water with 1 cup sugar until sugar is dissolved. Add 2 teaspoons almond extract and cool. Stir in 1 cup mixed fresh fruit.

APPLE PANCAKE

This recipe comes from the German wife of our New York apartment's superintendent. I often made these pancakes for my children's breakfast when they were young. When my daughter Loretta (as an adult) was terminally ill, I would ask her every night what she would like to eat before she went to sleep. She always asked for apple pancakes. Perhaps they reminded her of the times when I made them for her when she was a little girl. I was so glad that I had learned how to make apple pancakes so that I could please her.

½   **cup all-purpose flour**
½   **cup nonfat milk**
2   **eggs, separated**
dash of salt
1   **cup thin-sliced peeled apples**
¼   **cup vegetable oil**
sugar

PREPARATION
1. Combine flour, milk, egg yolks, and salt. Mix well. Add apples.

2. Beat egg whites until stiff. Fold in apple mixture.

COOKING
1. Preheat a wok, add vegetable oil, and heat over a high flame. When oil begins to smoke, reduce heat to medium.

2. Drop batter gently into hot oil, 1 to 2 heaping tablespoons at a time to make 4-inch round pancakes. Brown one side, then the other.

3. Sprinkle with sugar and serve warm.

SWEET WALNUT BROTH

For many Chinese people the walnut has great significance as a health food since it is considered especially good for the brain and for sound kidney function. It is interesting to note that the walnut is shaped much like the human brain!

My mother-in-law very frequently drank walnut broth—almost daily, as a matter of fact—and when she finally died at age 96 as the result of a fall, she had not one white hair on her head nor a wrinkle in her face.

2	cups walnuts
3½	cups water
1	cup sugar
3	Tbs. cornstarch dissolved in ¼ cup water
1	cup milk

PREPARATION
1. Soak walnuts in some hot water for an hour or longer. Skin, drain, and roast to golden brown.

2. Finely grind roasted walnuts in a food processor or blender. Add a little water if necessary to help grinding.

COOKING
1. In a pot, bring 3½ cups water to a boil. Add sugar and stir to dissolve.

2. Add walnut paste, stir thoroughly, and bring to a boil.

3. Add dissolved cornstarch, stirring constantly until thickened. Return to a boil.

4. Stir in milk, bringing almost to a boil. Serve.

Note: Peanuts or cashews may be substituted for the walnuts.

Makes 4 to 6 servings

SAUCES

Sauces play such an important role in Chinese cooking that I have decided to compile them in a section of their own.

There are two main categories of Chinese sauces: those that are used for dipping, usually for appetizers; and those that are more liquid in texture and used as part of the main dish. I am including some personal recipes for sauces in this section, in addition to the more popular Chinese sauces, many of which you will probably be familiar with. Ready-made sauces, which are available in Chinese groceries, include Chekiang vinegar, hoisin sauce, oyster sauce, plum sauce, soy sauce, and brown bean sauce. They are described in chapter 6.

While there are popular, standard Chinese sauces available on the market, many Chi-

nese cooks make their own with available ingredients. I suppose I am no different, because I like creating my own dipping and cooking sauces, as well as adapting existing ones, and these are used very often at my restaurant. You will find them easy to make and delicious, unusual accompaniments to many dishes.

WU'S MUSTARD

Used as a dip or accompaniment for appetizers and some meat dishes.

2   **tsp. powdered Colman's mustard**
2   **tsp. light soy sauce**
1   **tsp. sesame oil**

PREPARATION
In a china sauce dish mix ingredients to a creamy paste, adding water if necessary.

MADAME WU'S SPECIAL CHINESE DIP SAUCE

This sauce makes a good accompaniment to steamed fish, shrimp, or crab and also makes a good dip with less spicy chicken and pork dishes.

1	Tbs. wine vinegar
1	tsp. chopped scallion
1	tsp. chopped gingerroot
1	tsp. light soy sauce
1	tsp. oyster sauce
1	tsp. sesame oil
1	tsp. hot chili sauce or paste

PREPARATION
Mix ingredients to form a loose, smooth paste.

BARBECUE SAUCE MARINADE

Use for barbecued pork or beef,
particularly spareribs or short ribs.

3   Tbs. hoisin sauce
2   Tbs. catsup
2   cloves garlic, finely
      chopped
2   Tbs. sugar (optional)
2   tsp. dark soy sauce
1   tsp. light soy sauce

PREPARATION
Combine ingredients to make a
tangy-sweet marinade.

SWEET AND SOUR SAUCE

Goes well with seafood, poultry, or pork.

¾ cup catsup
¼ cup white vinegar
3 Tbs. sugar
reserved juice from canned
    pineapple chunks
½ cup chopped white onion
½ cup chopped green
    pepper
1 Tbs. cornstarch
    dissolved in 2 Tbs.
    water
1 8-ounce can pineapple
    chunks, juice reserved

COOKING
1. Combine catsup, vinegar, sugar, and pineapple juice. Pour into a preheated wok or skillet and cook over high heat.

2. When the mixture begins to boil, add onion and green pepper. Return to a boil.

3. Add the dissolved cornstarch. Stir well and add the pineapple chunks. When this mixture again reaches a boil, stir and serve.

GARDEN RESTAURANT BLACK BEAN SAUCE

Use with meat, poultry, fish, or shrimp.

2   Tbs. vegetable oil
2   Tbs. salted black beans
     put through a garlic
     press with 2 cloves
     garlic
¼   cup water
1   Tbs. dark soy sauce
1   tsp. red wine
1   tsp. cornstarch dissolved
     in 2 Tbs. water
½   tsp. salt

COOKING
1. Swirl oil around a preheated
   wok or deep skillet. Add the
   black bean and garlic mash
   and quick-fry over high heat
   until aroma rises.

2. Add remaining ingredients,
   stirring thoroughly.

WU'S TOMATO SAUCE

Best with beef, chicken, seafood, or pork.

1	Tbs. vegetable oil
1	medium-size yellow onion, coarsely chopped
1	cup coarsely chopped green peppers (optional)
2	cups coarsely chopped tomatoes
1	tsp. salt
¼	tsp. sugar
½	cup catsup

COOKING
1. Preheat a wok or deep skillet over high heat. Swirl in oil and quick-fry onions.

2. Add green peppers and stir-fry for 1 minute.

3. Add tomatoes, salt, and sugar; stir-fry for 3 minutes. Cover and cook for 1 minute.

4. Stir in catsup, and pour the sauce into a bowl for later use, or use immediately.

HOT AND SOUR SAUCE

Use to cook with meat, pork, fish, or vegetables.

2	Tbs. wine vinegar
1	Tbs. dark soy sauce
1	tsp. Tabasco sauce
1	tsp. sugar
¼	tsp. monosodium glutamate (optional)
¼	cup water

COOKING

1. In a small bowl, blend all the ingredients except water.

2. Add water and cook in a preheated wok or skillet, stirring well, until mixture boils and thickens slightly.

2

POPULAR CHINESE HERBS AND GOOD-HEALTH RECIPES

This book would not be complete without a chapter on the use of herbs in Chinese cooking. The Chinese believe that everything you eat should be good for you, and the cuisine is so intermingled with the natural forces of Yin and Yang that the Chinese housewife uses these forces to balance her family's diet for good health. Many of the roots and herbs which she uses as flavorings and supplements are the same as those recommended by Chinese herbalists.

Certain ingredients used in Chinese cooking are intended to further good health as well as good taste. They are meant as aids to digestion, blood circulation, the blood itself, strength, virility, femininity, and much more. Herbs go one step further. According to the Chinese, herbs are frequently used as medication, and will remedy all kinds of disturbances, from arthritis to insomnia, from stomach ailments to respiratory disorders.

Chinese herbalists, however, do not claim to cure anything. Rather, they provide supplements for what is lacking in the body. They believe that herbs are a part of nature's very own plan to provide us with a complete, wholesome way to care for ourselves and to rid ourselves of the ailments that may beset us from time to time. The importance of herbs in Chinese culture and life-style is part of a long tradition and herbs are regarded and accepted as a necessary part of life. As the great scholar Lin Yutang said, the Chinese do not draw any distinction between food and medicine. What is good for the body is medicine and at the same time, food.

All this reminds me of an illness I had a long time ago, when I was growing up in China. I had been severely ill for many months and while the doctors were working on the diagnosis and deciding whether or not I should be sent abroad for treatment, my grandfather tried to build up my strength with a special concoction of his own. He gave me large doses of a concentrated chicken broth with ginseng. It made a very rich Yang food, which I could take because, as my grandfather pointed out, I had a Yin body system.

As the brew was a strong tonic, I was supposed to drink only the liquid and not eat the chicken or the ginseng root. My maid did not know this, however, and, realizing that the brew was as nutritious as it was costly, she ate everything I left behind, including all the chicken meat and the ginseng root. The next thing the poor maid knew, her face had become red and swollen. She was, of course, very upset, but my grandfather knew at once what had happened. She had reacted to the rich Yang brew which did not agree with what he called her "Yang system." I suppose too much of a good thing isn't really good at all, but that tonic really did help me through those long months, until I was able to come to the United States for treatment.

So, keeping in mind our thoughts on health and longevity, I would like to include a few ancient and traditional recipes for some of the more popular brews and hope that you will find them as refreshing and invigorating as we Chinese do.

Please note that the more unusual ingredients (such as ginseng, deer horn, and tang kuei) are available at Chinese groceries or Chinese herbalists.

Also note that the following recipes are cooked in an earthenware steamer, which traditionally is a covered pot with a central chimney through which steam circulates throughout the pot.

GINSENG WITH SQUAB

In China this is called a "lifesaving" tonic.

2   **squabs**
2   **ounces ginseng root, rinsed**
2   **slices gingerroot**
3   **cups water**

COOKING

1. Combine ingredients in an earthen steamer and cover.

2. Brew over low heat for 3 to 4 hours. Consume the liquid only.

DEER-HORN TONIC

Herbal tonics are used in winter, because they raise the body temperature and increase circulation. Use of these tonics in the summer is considered a waste, as the body would lose all the benefits through perspiration.

1½   pounds cock, skinned
4   cups water
2   slices gingerroot
6   dried red dates, pitted
         and cleaned
1   ounce shaved deer horn

PREPARATION
1. Chop chicken into 4 pieces and parboil for 10 minutes. Discard water.

2. Boil 4 cups water vigorously and set aside to cool.

COOKING
1. Pour cooled boiled water into an earthenware steamer. Add chicken and remaining ingredients.

2. Cover and brew over low heat for 3 hours.

CHING PO LEUNG SOUP

This soup is common in most Chinese homes. Even my cooks at the restaurant make it two or three times a month for the employees. The Chinese believe strongly that it is health giving because it has a balance of Yin and Yang. The packaged contents, available at Chinese groceries, include dry lily buds, pearl barley, lotus seeds, discorea, dry longan, fox nuts, and polygonatum.

1	package Ching Po Leung ingredients
1	pound lean pork
4	cups boiling water

PREPARATION
1. Soak packaged ingredients 2 to 3 hours.

2. Trim pork of any fat and cut into 1"-×-2"chunks.

COOKING
1. Combine all ingredients in an earthenware pot.

2. Brew for 4 hours over low heat. Serve hot.

BREWED TANG KUEI AND CHICKEN

This is an ancient herbal recipe. In China it is used mostly by women who have just given birth, or who have reached menopause. My sister-in-law who lives in Hong Kong claims that Western women take hormone pills that can have harmful side effects, but tang kuei never has side effects to worry about.

1½   **pounds cock, skinned**
4   **cups thin-sliced tang kuei, rinsed**
2   **slices gingerroot, crushed**
1   **Tbs. dry sherry**
3   **cups boiling water**

PREPARATION
Chop chicken into 4 pieces and parboil for 10 minutes. Discard water.

COOKING
1. Add chicken, tang kuei, ginger, and sherry to a pot of boiling water.

2. Cover and simmer over low heat for 5 hours. If water evaporates during cooking, add more as necessary. Should be taken hot.

PIGS' FEET AND GINGER IN VINEGAR

This is a traditional concoction for women after giving birth. It is supposed to help remove any placenta remaining inside the womb. Since it is so delicious, it is usually served to all members of the family and guests who visit.

6   **pigs' feet, cut into 2-inch rounds**
1   **pound young gingerroot, peeled**
1   **24-ounce bottle dark Chekiang vinegar**
1   **pound light brown sugar**
12   **eggs, hard-boiled**

PREPARATION
1. Wash pigs' feet, put them in a large pot, and cover with water.

2. Bring to a boil and boil for 5 minutes. Drain and set aside.

COOKING
1. In a large pot, preferably earthenware, combine pigs' feet, ginger, and vinegar. Bring to a boil and simmer for 3 to 4 hours, or until pigs' feet are tender.

2. Add sugar and hard-boiled eggs; simmer for 30 minutes. Serve hot.

3

BANQUET
RECIPES
FROM THE
PAN HSI
RESTAURANT
AND THE
JING JIANG
HOTEL

It gives me great pleasure to be able to include banquet recipes from the Pan Hsi Restaurant in Kwangchow and the Jing Jiang Hotel in Shanghai. All of the recipes were demonstrated with great success in my restaurant by teams of chefs from these two famous establishments. First was a team of four men and two women from the Pan Hsi, led by Master Chef Lo Kwan, here on an official tour of the United States by invitation of the Chinese Culinary Institute and the Collegiate International Trading Corporation in New York. I was delighted to have the chefs demonstrate at my restaurant for their West Coast engagement.

On opening night, Lo Kwan led his chefs in an impressive parade of their exquisite and picturesque work. Each platter of food was arranged to look like a phoenix, rooster, heron, or some other exotic bird or flower. The long ovation my illustrious guests generously gave the chefs was proof of their appreciation for the extraordinary efforts taken by the team in preparing, decorating, and serving their prize dishes.

In the three days that the Pan Hsi chefs were at my restaurant, they prepared and served four banquets and two dim sum lunches. Both lunches were benefits for the Loretta Wu Wong Scholarship Fund, set up in memory of my dear, late daughter, Loretta. The first eight recipes in this section are dishes executed by that talented team.

The Pan Hsi chefs were so successful that I felt it would be even more exciting to bring out another team of chefs from China, this time featuring a different style of cooking. The opportunity came in 1981, when my husband King and I went to Beijing to attend the state funeral of our dear friend, Madame Sun Yat-sen.

While we were in China, we attended a state banquet held at the famous Jing Jiang Hotel, in Shanghai. During dinner, I found myself seated next to the mayor and mentioned to him the successful tour undertaken by the Pan Hsi chefs the year before. To the delight of the mayor, who thought it was a wonderful idea, I suggested that perhaps a team of Jing Jiang chefs could do the same thing.

Nothing really came of it, though, until a year later, when we returned to China for the first anniversary of Madame Sun's death and the official opening ceremony of Madame Sun's house as a state museum. Again, the mayor of Shanghai hosted a banquet at the Jing Jiang Hotel. This time, I found myself seated next to Mr. Yen, who was the head of the hotel industry in China, and so I very seriously broached the question again, asking if he would give his permission for the chefs to come to the United States. It was an exciting moment when he said immediately, "Yes!"

And so it was in the week beginning December 5, 1982, coinciding with the twenty-second anniversary of my Garden Restaurant, chefs from the Jing Jiang Hotel prepared no less than six banquets in as many days. Led by Master Chef Hong Peng Xiang, who came out of retirement for the occasion, the team prepared and served twenty-one gourmet dishes, each with a fascinating name and taste. There was Cold Platter with Eight Sisters, Golden Shrimp in a Lantern, Jing Jiang Silver Threads, The Lake Yields Its Treasure, Pearls Hidden under the Crab, Medals from the Chef, Four Winds in a Garden, Birds on a Cloud, and more. Even the dessert was an unusual dish of fried milk, christened Shanghai Goddess.

It was a very hectic week for the Jing Jiang chefs, who were actually working above capacity, but they very good-humoredly went about their work, always jovial and unflustered. It was a pleasure working with them. Their delicious dishes made a great impression on me, and I would like to share four of them with you. They constitute the end of this chapter.

LOVELY FANTASIA

½	pound canned bamboo shoots, shredded
1	beef tongue weighing at least 1 pound, cooked and thin-sliced
¼	cup thin-sliced cooked Virginia ham
1	thousand-year-old egg, thin-sliced
5	cooked prawns, thin-sliced
¼	cup thin-sliced cooked chicken breast
¼	cup thin-sliced barbecued or roasted duck meat
¼	cup thin-sliced cooked chicken livers
6	quail eggs, boiled and thin-sliced
¼	cup thin-sliced cooked Chinese sausage
¼	package sheet-style dried seaweed, thin-sliced

PREPARATION

1. Arrange the shredded bamboo shoots on a platter to sketch out a design of your choice, such as a phoenix, peacock, rooster, lobster, or butterfly. Use your imagination.

2. Using the remaining ingredients as an artist would use a palette of colors and textures, arrange them on top of the sketched-out design in layers to make a realistic and colorful display. Serve cold.

Makes 10 small servings

Remember that this recipe and those that follow in this section are dishes for banquets at which many courses are served. Portions of each course are small.

WHITE RABBIT ON GREEN LAWN

¼ cup minced raw shrimp
2 Tbs. canned shredded
  bamboo shoots
1 Tbs. minced water
  chestnuts
2 Tbs. vegetable oil
1 tsp. light soy sauce
½ tsp. salt
1 pound wheat starch
1 Tbs. diced ham
1 bunch parsley

PREPARATION

1. Combine shrimp, bamboo shoots, water chestnuts, oil, soy sauce, and salt. Mix well. Divide into 10 portions.

2. Add enough boiling water to wheat starch to make a dough. (Leftover dough keeps well in the refrigerator.) Knead until smooth and shape into 10 flat discs.

3. Wrap these around the filling and mold to resemble rabbits. The finished rabbits are 1½ to 2 inches in length.

4. Use diced ham for the eyes.

5. Garnish with parsley.

Makes 10 small servings

SWEET SOUP OF SILVER EARS AND QUAIL EGGS

1	cup silver ears
¼	cup rock candy
3	cups boiling water
12	canned quail eggs

PREPARATION
1. Wash and clean silver ears. Soak in some water until swollen.

2. Dissolve rock candy in the boiling water. Filter the solution.

COOKING
1. Put silver ears and rock candy solution in an earthenware Chinese steamer. Steam for about 1½ hours.

2. Add quail eggs and steam for 5 to 10 minutes. Serve hot.

Makes 10 small servings

SCALLOPS ON BLACK MOSS

12	dried scallops
2	ounces dried black moss
3	Tbs. vegetable oil
1	slice gingerroot
1	scallion
1	Tbs. white wine
1	tsp. light soy sauce
2	cups chicken broth
5	cloves garlic
1	tsp. cornstarch

PREPARATION

1. Soak scallops in cool water for 15 minutes. Cut out hard parts and place scallops in a heatproof bowl.

2. Wash black moss thoroughly and soak in hot water to cover for 10 minutes.

COOKING

1. Preheat a wok. Add oil, ginger, scallion, wine, soy sauce, and black moss. Stir-fry for 1 minute.

2. Add chicken broth and stir-fry for 1 minute.

3. Strain sauce into a bowl and reserve.

4. Place cooked black moss on top of scallops and add garlic. Place bowl in a steamer. Steam for 1 hour.

5. Thicken the reserved sauce (step 3) with cornstarch and add any additional liquid from the steaming.

TO SERVE

Invert bowl of scallops and black moss on a platter so the scallops are on top of the moss. The dish should resemble a hat with a fur brim. Pour the thickened sauce on top. Serve hot.

Makes 10 small servings

ABALONE AND DUCK GOLD AND SILVER THREADS

5	Tbs. vegetable oil
½	cup thin-sliced roast duck
½	cup thin-sliced canned abalone
1	Tbs. white wine
1	tsp. light soy sauce
1	slice gingerroot, thin-sliced
½	cup soaked and thin-sliced dried black mushrooms
1	carrot, thin-sliced
1	Tbs. dark soy sauce
½	tsp. salt
½	tsp. sugar
1	red bell pepper, thin-sliced
1	green bell pepper, thin-sliced
4	center celery stalks, thin-sliced
1	cup trimmed bean sprouts

fried rice noodles (see **Shredded Chicken Salad, page 72**)

COOKING

1. In a preheated wok or deep skillet, add 2 tablespoons oil. When hot, stir-fry duck and abalone for 1 minute.

2. Add wine and light soy sauce; stir-fry for 1 minute. Remove from wok and set aside.

3 Clean wok. Heat remaining 3 tablespoons oil. Add ginger, black mushrooms, and carrot; stir-fry for 2 minutes.

4. Add dark soy sauce, salt, and sugar; stir-fry for 1 minute.

5. Add red and green peppers, celery, and bean sprouts. Stir-fry for 1 to 2 minutes.

6. Return duck and abalone to the wok; stir-fry for 1 minute. Serve hot.

7. Garnish with crisp fried rice noodles.

Makes 10 small servings

DEEP-FRIED "PHOENIX-TAIL" PRAWNS

16	prawns
½	tsp. salt
½	tsp. sugar
1	tsp. rice wine
1	tsp. sesame oil
1	tsp. chopped gingerroot
1	tsp. chopped scallion
2	Tbs. flour plus extra for dusting prawns
12	egg whites
1	Tbs. cornstarch
1	cup bread crumbs

3 to 4 cups vegetable oil
Worcestershire sauce
    (optional)
salt and pepper to taste
    (optional)

PREPARATION

1. Shell prawns, leaving tails intact. Cut off heads and discard. Split down back but do not cut through. Remove intestinal vein. Wash, drain, and dry on paper towels.

2. Combine salt, sugar, rice wine, sesame oil, ginger, and scallion and marinate prawns in mixture for 2 minutes.

3. Dust marinated prawns with a little flour.

4. Whip egg whites until foamy and thick. Stir in 2 tablespoons flour and cornstarch. Mix well.

5. Hold each prawn by the tail and dip into egg-white batter. Pat with bread crumbs.

COOKING

1. Preheat a wok and add vegetable oil. Heat oil to 350°F. Deep-fry prawns until golden brown.

2. Serve on a platter with Worcestershire sauce and pepper and salt, or use your favorite sauce (chapter 1).

Makes 10 small servings

PEAR-SHAPED DUMPLINGS

2 Tbs. wheat starch
½ pound potatoes, boiled
and mashed

FILLING
3 Tbs. vegetable oil
¼ cup diced barbecued
pork
¼ cup diced cooked
chicken
2 Tbs. diced cooked shrimp
2 Tbs. soaked and diced
dried black
mushrooms
1 tsp. white wine
1 tsp. light soy sauce
1 tsp. sesame oil
½ tsp. salt
½ tsp. curry powder
1 tsp. cornstarch dissolved
in 2 tsp. water

1 egg, beaten
½ cup fine bread crumbs
4 cups vegetable oil
1 slice ham, cut into ¼"-×-
½" pieces

PREPARATION
1. Add enough boiling water to
wheat starch to combine it
with mashed potatoes.

2. Prepare filling: Add oil to a
preheated wok. When hot
briefly stir-fry pork, chicken,
shrimp, and mushrooms with
white wine, soy sauce,
sesame oil, and salt. Add
curry powder and dissolved
cornstarch.

3. Divide potatoes into 16 parts
and mold each around some
of the filling into the shape
of a pear.

4. Brush each pear with egg,
then dust with bread crumbs.

COOKING
1. Heat oil in preheated wok.
Deep-fry pears until golden
brown.

2. Insert pieces of ham as
"stems." Serve hot.

Makes 10 small servings.

BUDDHA JUMP OVER THE WALL

This dish is famous in Fukien Province. Because it must be steamed overnight, its delicious aroma fills the night air. It once kept a nearby monastery of Buddhist monks awake all night. Even Buddha was not able to stand the wonderful aroma and he jumped over the wall. This dish contains so many elegant and nourishing ingredients that it is as good for you as it is to taste, and very expensive. Prepared in Hong Kong, it costs between $2,000 to $3,000 H.K. (about $500 U.S.), and takes 48 hours to prepare.

1	large Chinese or Virginia ham
1	stewing chicken
1	shark's fin
4	dried abalone
10	dried scallops
1	Chinese white cabbage
1	slice gingerroot
rice paper	

PREPARATION

1. Clean ham, cover with water, and soak overnight. Drain and cut into ¼-inch slices, then cut into 2-inch pieces.

2. Clean chicken, skin, and remove excess fat. Cut chicken into 10 pieces.

3. Clean shark's fin, cover with water, and soak overnight. Drain. Boil in water 3 to 4 hours. Drain. Rinse lightly with cold water.

4. Cover abalone with water and soak overnight. Drain and slice into 2-inch pieces.

5. Clean scallops, remove hard parts, cover with water, and soak for 1 hour.

6. Clean cabbage, cut in half, and divide into 6 pieces.

COOKING

1. Fill a large (about 18 inches) earthenware pot with water and bring to a boil.

2. Starting with the ham, layer the ingredients in the pot, including the sliced gingerroot.

3. Tightly wrap the pot, including the cover, with rice paper. Reduce heat and simmer overnight.

Makes 10 servings.

PEARLS HIDDEN UNDER THE CRAB

1	large crab, freshly steamed in its shell
¼	pound crab meat
4	Tbs. vegetable oil
2	scallions, chopped
1	slice gingerroot, crushed
2	hard-boiled egg yolks, mashed
12	canned quail eggs

PREPARATION

1. Remove legs from crab, keeping them intact, and set aside. Separate shell from crab. Wash and clean top shell and set aside.

2. Remove meat remaining inside crab shell and add to ¼ pound crab meat. Shred all meat evenly.

COOKING

1. Preheat a wok, add oil, and when hot lightly cook shredded crab meat, scallions, and ginger for 1 minute.

2. Add egg yolks and stir for 1 minute.

3. Add quail eggs and stir for 1 more minute.

TO SERVE

Place crab meat and eggs in the center of a platter. Place cleaned crab shell on top and arrange the crab legs as they were originally so that the crab looks natural. Serve immediately.

Makes 10 small servings.

GOLDEN SHRIMP IN A LANTERN

1 **pound shrimp**

SAUCE
¼ **cup catsup**
1 **Tbs. Tabasco sauce**
1 **Tbs. dry sherry**
1 **tsp. light soy sauce**
1 **tsp. honey**

¼ **cup vegetable oil**
1 **Tbs. crushed gingerroot**
2 **Tbs. chopped scallion**
1 **Tbs. cornstarch
    dissolved in 2 Tbs.
    water**
**2-foot square heavy-duty clear
    cellophane**
**24-inch strips of red ribbon and
    green ribbon**

PREPARATION
1. Peel and devein shrimp and butterfly-cut.

2. Combine sauce ingredients in a bowl and set aside.

COOKING
1. Preheat a wok or deep skillet to high (375°F). Add vegetable oil, ginger, and shrimp. Stir-fry for 2 minutes, or until shrimp turns pink.

2. Add scallion and sauce; stir-fry for 1 minute.

3. When sauce is boiling, quickly stir in dissolved cornstarch.

TO SERVE
Place the cellophane over a deep bowl and scoop shrimp on top. Carefully bring the four corners of the cellophane together and tie with a ribbon. This forms the "lantern" with the red shrimp "glowing" inside. Place on a serving platter. Serve hot.

Makes 10 small servings.

FOUR WINDS IN A GARDEN

3	Tbs. vegetable oil
1	slice gingerroot
12	small white turnips
12	small Chinese white cabbage hearts
¼	cup chicken broth
12	canned baby corn cobs, drained
12	canned button mushrooms, drained
1	Tbs. cornstarch dissolved in 2 Tbs. water

COOKING

1. Preheat a wok and add vegetable oil and ginger. When oil is hot, add turnips and stir-fry for 2 minutes.

2. Add cabbage and stir-fry for 1 minute.

3. Add chicken broth, cover, and cook for 2 minutes.

4. Add corn cobs and mushrooms; stir for 1 minute.

5. Leaving the liquid in the wok, arrange the vegetables on a platter like an open fan, with the corn cobs around the edge, overlapped with the cabbage hearts, then a row of turnips, and in the center the mushrooms.

6. Bring the liquid in the wok to a boil and add the dissolved cornstarch.

7. Stir and pour over the vegetables. Serve hot.

Makes 10 small servings.

SHANGHAI GODDESS (Deep-Fried Milk)

1¼   **cups chicken broth**
1   **Tbs. butter**
½   **cup coconut milk**
2   **Tbs. evaporated milk**
5   **Tbs. cornstarch**
      dissolved in ¼ cup
      chicken broth

BATTER
½   **cup all-purpose flour**
¼   **cup cornstarch**
½   **tsp. baking powder**
1   **egg**
½   **cup water**
1   **Tbs. vegetable oil**

1   **cup vegetable oil**
sugar

PREPARATION

1. Bring chicken broth to a gentle boil. Add butter, coconut milk, and evaporated milk. Stir well.

2. Remove from heat and stir in dissolved cornstarch. Stir constantly over low heat until the mixture thickens. Bring to a gentle boil.

3. Pour milk mixture into shallow 6"-square or rectangular (6"-×-8") pan. The depth of mixture should be about ¾ to 1 inch. Let set in refrigerator overnight, then cut into 1"-×-1"-×-2" bars.

4. Prepare batter: Mix all ingredients to smooth consistency.

COOKING

1. Preheat a wok and add oil. When hot, dip milk bars in batter and deep-fry until golden brown on all sides. Keep oil gently boiling during deep-frying.

3. Serve fried milk with sugar for dipping.

Makes 10 small servings.

4

CHINESE FESTIVAL RECIPES

Like everyone else, we Chinese have a variety of different foods and dishes which we prepare and serve on festive occasions. Feasting is a part of Chinese culture and we take great pride in producing difficult and tasty dishes and exotic sweetmeats for special times of the year. Many, if not all, of the dishes have special significance and are prepared as part of a tradition. There is usually a reason or legend behind each dish. As a child, I loved listening to the stories my grandfather told me about Chinese festivals and why certain foods, cakes, and sweets were prepared only for those certain days. I remember my grandmother telling me not to come into the kitchen when she prepared all those lovely goodies for Chinese New Year, in case I should say something silly and make the gods angry!

Of course, festival dishes are good at any time of the year, and so I am featuring some of the more popular and simpler ones for you to try, together with the tradition behind them. The three most important festivals in the Chinese calendar are Chinese New Year; the May 5th, or Dragon Boat, Festival; and the Mooncake Festival, all of which provide us with an opportunity to make the traditional dishes not prepared at other times of the year.

CHINESE NEW YEAR

This is the most important festival of all as it marks the end of the old and the beginning of the new. So it is up to each and every person to try his or her best to settle all debts, try to patch up old quarrels, do acts of kindness, clean his home, dress himself well, so that the New Year will be happy, bright, and prosperous. Since it is such an important event, many households spend months preparing for it, so that the celebration will be joyful, noisy, and warm. After all, Chinese New Year only comes around once in every twelve months!

One of the traditions for Chinese New Year is that anyone who is away from his or her family should return home three days before the New Year. This is still observed in some families, even today. There were no holidays in old China, and the only time that people were allowed to forget their work was at Chinese New Year, when it was the custom to spend two weeks celebrating. Husbands, fathers, and sons who worked away from home made sure that they returned to their families in good time for the festivities. The New Year has remained a traditional time for family members to reunite. Many still come from far and wide just to keep this custom, as family unity will ensure the continual progress of the universe. This is in keeping with the concept of the complete Yin and Yang.

Some of the dishes prepared for Chinese New Year include the famous Eight Precious Duck, Rice Candy, Chinese New Year Sausages, Rice Cakes, and Egg Roll Biscuits. Smoked meats are also very popular during this time, and you will find many shops in Chinatown selling sugar-cured sliced pork, beef, chicken, duck, and fish. I remember Grandfather used to burn huge quantities of sugarcane to smoke his own meats, and I must say they always tasted best to me!

You will find the recipe for Eight Precious Duck in chapter 1, POULTRY, while I am including two special Chinese New Year recipes in this chapter.

CHINESE NEW YEAR RICE CAKES (Jien Dai)

Jien Dai are a delicious New Year treat. Sweet and tasty, they represent all that the New Year should bring. Their roundness signifies the completeness of the family and the unity within it. Again, the concept of Yin and Yang is present. But as children, we only knew that Jien Dai was something you could never get enough of. Today, as a calorie- and health-conscious adult, I would never want to overindulge!

½   cup brown sugar
⅔   cup boiling water
8   ounces glutinous rice
        flour
8   ounces black bean paste
½   cup white sesame seeds
vegetable oil

PREPARATION

1. Dissolve brown sugar in the boiling water and continue to boil until syrupy. Remove from the heat and slowly stir into the glutinous rice flour, until a pliable dough is formed.

2. Roll dough into a long strip, about 1 inch in diameter. Cut off 1-inch sections and roll each section into a ball with the palms of your hands.

3. Flatten a ball of dough in the palm of your hand. Place a little black bean paste on it and then fold the dough over and around it, finally rolling it into a smooth dumpling with the palms of your hands.

4. Roll the dumpling in the sesame seeds until the entire surface is covered.

COOKING

In a preheated wok or deep skillet, add oil. When hot, place balls in oil and deep-fry over medium heat until they rise to the surface and the cake is golden brown. Serve hot.

Makes about 20 balls

NEW YEAR RICE CANDY

Although this was a New Year treat, rice candy was popular throughout the year.

1	cup white rice, or 1 pound puffed rice cereal
¾	cup sugar
½	cup water
¼	tsp. vanilla (optional)

PREPARATION
If using rice, soak in water overnight. Dry on paper towels and heat in a wok or heavy pot until the rice puffs up. Remove from heat immediately and set aside.

COOKING
1. Combine sugar and water and boil for 7 to 10 minutes over medium-high heat, until a thick syrup forms.

2. Flavor with vanilla, if desired, and pour into a well-greased cookie pan or baking dish. Quickly stir the puffed rice into the syrup, mixing well. Pack the rice down firmly and leave to cool.

3. When set, cut into 1"-×-2" bars and serve. Store in an airtight container to retain crispness.

DRAGON BOAT FESTIVAL

The next important festival in the Chinese year falls on May 5th, and is commonly known as the Dragon Boat Festival. Special glutinous rice cakes, wrapped in ti leaves, are the main festive fare.

The legend behind this festival celebrates a high-ranking government official, named Wut Yuen, who lived in the Chou Dynasty. Because he was hard working, good, and kind, he was favored by the Emperor, and because he was not a proud man, the common people liked him, too. Lower-ranking officials, however, were extremely jealous of Wut Yuen's position and favor with the Emperor. They carried false tales to the Emperor and in time succeeded in making the Emperor angry with his favorite. Poor Wut Yuen was stripped of his power and asked to leave the Emperor's court. Feeling sad and indignant, Wut Yuen tied a huge rock to his waist and jumped into the river.

The people were very sad when they found out what had happened, and they set out in their boats to search the river for their beloved official. They could not find him, so they did what they thought was best: They made him special food wrapped in leaves and threw it into the river, so that he would never starve in his watery world.

Then Wut Yuen appeared to a villager in a dream and told him that the food was being eaten by the dragons that lived under the river. He suggested that next time the people should wrap the food in colorful paper and beat gongs when they threw the packages into the river, because bright colors and loud noises were known to chase dragons away. From that time on, people used plenty of colored ribbons and paper when they rushed out in their boats to see who would be the first to give the great man his food.

So today, the Dragon Boat Festival is celebrated in honor of this good and kind official, and the Dragon Boat Races commemorate the search parties and the early rush to the spot where Wut Yuen drowned so many hundreds of years ago. The special rice cakes which are eaten at this time commemorate the food first prepared for him by the villagers. The delicious variety of these cakes is the main reason why the Dragon Boat Festival is still enjoyed by Chinese all over the world.

DRAGON'S DELIGHT (Haahm Joong)

1	pound glutinous rice
2	tsp. salt
3	Tbs. vegetable oil
1	cup lotus seeds
¼	tsp. baking soda
1	dried black mushroom
1	9-ounce package frozen green peas, cooked
8	ounces Chinese roast pork, diced
4	ounces slab bacon, diced
48	dried ti leaves

PREPARATION

1. Soak rice overnight in cold water. Drain at least 30 minutes and mix in the salt and oil.

2. Boil lotus seeds and baking soda in water for 15 minutes. Drain and scrape off as much of the brown husk as possible, then soak the lotus seeds in cold water until remaining husks loosen on their own.

3. Soak mushroom for 15 minutes and fine-dice.

4. Combine all ingredients, except ti leaves, and set aside.

5. Ready leaves for wrapping by soaking in cold water until pliable—at least ½ hour. Fill and wrap.

COOKING

In a large pot, boil for 3 to 4 hours.

Makes 12 Haahm Joong

DRAGON'S TOOTH (Tiem Joong)

2	pounds glutinous rice
1	Tbs. vegetable oil
1	pound canned black bean paste
48	dried ti leaves

PREPARATION

1. Soak rice overnight in cold water. Drain 30 minutes, until dry. Mix rice and oil together and set aside.

2. Roll bean paste into a long strip, about 1 inch in diameter. Cut into twenty-four 3-inch lengths and flatten each slightly.

3. Place some rice on a ti leaf. Cover with a portion of bean paste, and cover this with more rice. Then wrap.

COOKING

In a pot, boil in lightly salted water for 3 to 4 hours until completely cooked.

Makes 24 Tiem Joong

MOONCAKE FESTIVAL

Another important festival for the Chinese is the Mooncake Festival, or the Festival of the August Moon. This festival falls on the fifteenth day of the eighth month, when the moon is big and at its brightest. This also coincides with the harvest, which, if you have been hard working, should be bountiful. The moon was the Queen of Heaven in Chinese folklore, and she governed the tides of the river, which in turn affected the crops. So each year, the farm folk paid their respects to the moon, thanking her for their harvest with happy picnics and festivities held under her light.

There are many ancient legends regarding the Goddess of Heaven. One of the prettiest tells a story that took place about 2500 B.C. A fairy queen of the West, Suy Wong Mo, gave a measure of the drink from the Fountain of Youth to a handsome young chieftain named Hao Yeh. Unfortunately, the elixir was stolen by his beautiful wife, Sheung Aw, who wanted to live forever. He was extremely angry with her, and she ran away to the moon to escape his anger. Once there, the merciful gods of heaven took pity on her and changed her into a toad, so that no one would recognize her. So that her great beauty would live on, it is said that Sheung Aw's outline may be traced upon the surface of the August moon.

During the Mooncake Festival, all the cake shops and restaurants in Chinatown sell the very popular and delicate mooncakes that mark this festival. Shaped like the moon, they are made of a flaky dough of rice flour, each layer made separately. The dough is slightly sweet and very rich and is seldom prepared at home, as it is very difficult to make. Mooncakes come in a wide variety, each filled differently—with meat and mushrooms, bean paste, chestnut paste, salted, whole yolk of egg, mashed lotus seeds, sesame seeds, melon seeds. Just this year, a friend of mine saw a brand-new variety being advertised all over Singapore, containing a special chestnut-chocolate filling and a chocolate-almond truffle filling. Even tradition seems to move ahead with the times!

Since mooncakes are so difficult to make, I will not include them in this chapter. Instead, I *will* give you the recipes of some of the less complicated fillings, which you can use with your own flaky pastry or doughnut dough. These are rich and not by any means health foods, but they certainly are fun!

Use approximately 2 tablespoons of any of these fillings for each pastry.

CHESTNUT AND RED BEAN STUFFING

1   pound chestnuts, roasted
        and shelled
2   Tbs. sugar
2   Tbs. sesame seeds
1   8-ounce can sweet red
        bean paste

PREPARATION
1. Mash chestnuts thoroughly
   and add sesame seeds and
   sugar. Mix well.

2. Add bean paste and mix into
   a thick paste. Use for filling
   as desired.

CHESTNUT CREAM FILLING

1   pound chestnuts, roasted
    and shelled
¼   cup butter or margarine
1¼   cups powdered sugar
1   tsp. vanilla, brandy, or
    rum to taste
½   cup whipping cream
milk (optional)

PREPARATION
1. Mash chestnuts thoroughly
   and cream in butter and
   sugar.

2. Stir in vanilla.

3. Add whipping cream and mix
   to a smooth, thick, creamy
   paste. Add milk if necessary.
   Use as desired.

CHICKEN CASHEW FILLING

2	Tbs. hoisin sauce
2	Tbs. light soy sauce
1	Tbs. cornstarch
1	Tbs. red wine or sherry (optional)
2	pounds chicken breast, boned and diced
4	Tbs. vegetable oil
8	ounces raw cashew nuts
3 to 4	cloves garlic, finely chopped
½	large white onion, finely chopped
1	slice gingerroot, finely chopped
1	Tbs. dark soy sauce
1	large can mushrooms, sliced
1	9-ounce package frozen green peas
sugar to taste	

PREPARATION

1. Combine hoisin sauce, 1 tablespoon light soy sauce, cornstarch, and wine.

2. Briefly marinate chicken. Set aside.

COOKING

1. Preheat a wok or deep skillet and add 2 tablespoons oil. When hot, briefly stir-fry cashews. Remove and set aside.

2. In the same wok heat the remaining 2 tablespoons oil. Add in quick succession, stirring briefly after each addition, the garlic, onion, and ginger.

3. Add chicken and cook until it gives the appearance of being roasted.

4. Add dark soy sauce, remaining tablespoon light soy, and mushrooms. Cook briefly.

5. Add green peas and stir until bright green.

6. Return cashews to wok and sprinkle with sugar to taste. Use as desired.

5

CHINESE
TEAS

The Chinese regard their tea the way the French regard their Cognac. To us, tea is a tradition, a way of life. Tea is considered to be good for the digestion because it dissolves grease and oil. This is why traditional Chinese will put tea instead of water into the finger bowl. As a child in my grandfather's house, we used to wash our hands in tea after eating fresh-cooked crab with our fingers. All the grease and fishy smell disappeared like magic.

You will find a cup or glass of tea with every Chinese meal, at every Chinese restaurant, anywhere in the world. In fact, every Chinese household, large or small, wealthy or poor, will have a hot pot of tea sitting in a tea-caddy basket, ready for the unexpected visitor. It is offered to the guest as a gesture of friendship and welcome; the guest will accept it gracefully and drink at least some of it, as a mark of respect to his or her host. It amuses me to see Chinese tea-caddy baskets being used here as ladies' purses!

The Chinese, like the Japanese, have their tea ceremony, but ours is usually part of special or festive occasions, like weddings and Chinese New Year. A Chinese bride will, immediately after the wedding ceremony, go to the home of her husband's parents and prepare and serve them tea in fine porcelain cups. This is a tradition that goes back for many hundreds of years and many Chinese families still observe this custom today. At the wedding reception, the bride will visit each table and serve tea to her guests, who will drink it as a toast to her long life and happiness and then present her with red envelopes or *hung pao*, containing good-luck money or *li see*.

On Chinese New Year Day, all children, married and unmarried, prepare and serve tea to their parents, grandparents, uncles, and aunts, as a mark of respect and good wishes, for tea is linked with good luck and prosperity. It "washes away" the old and welcomes the new.

There are as many as 250 varieties of Chinese tea, the most popular being jasmine and oolong. At my restaurant, I like to serve a blend of green and black teas. This is very popular with my guests because the mixture has the wonderful fragrance of green tea, with the richer color of the black. A list and description of the different Chinese teas follows.

POPULAR CHINESE TEAS

Ching Yuen
A black tea from Canton, which is preferred as a late-night beverage with light snacks.

Chrysanthemum
A flowered tea from Chekiang Province, made from the petals of the chrysanthemum. It is usually served after meals.

Heung Peen
A green tea, whose name literally means "fragrant petals," from Chinkiang Province. It is usually served at small parties for relatives or close friends.

Hung Cha
A red tea from Fukien Province that is most often served in Chinese restaurants in the United States. It has the misfortune of being the tea which was dumped in the harbor at the Boston Tea Party.

Jasmine
This very popular variety of red tea comes from both Formosa and Fukien Province. It is a combination of jasmine flowers and JUN JING. Jasmine tea is fragrant and delicious.

Jun Jing
The Chinese name for "Dragon Well Tea." From Chinkiang Province, it is one of the finest green teas, being light in color, with a mild, refreshing flavor.

Keemun
Another very popular red tea, it comes from both Kiangsi and Anhwei Provinces. The most famous of Chinese teas, it is spicy, but smooth and delicate.

Lapsang Souchong
A well-known favorite with Chinese tea drinkers. It is a black variety and comes from Yunan Province. It is very strong and has a pronounced smoky flavor.

Lichee (Litchi)
A flowered black tea from Formosa, flavored with lichee leaf. It is faintly sweet to the taste.

Lo Cha
Another flowered tea from Formosa. It is a combination of oolong tea and lichee flowers and is served to renew ties of friendship.

Mei Kwei
A black rose tea from Formosa, made with dried rosebuds.

Ngun Jum
Literally translated, the name of this tea means "silver needle." This Cantonese tea is served at special banquets.

Oolong
The famous Formosan "Black Dragon Tea." Its flavor is a combination of green and black tea and it is served at any time.

Poo Nay
A black tea, considered a powerful tonic, from Fukien Province.

Su Tong
A black tea from Fukien Province, generally served as a late evening beverage.

Swong Yuck
A green tea from Hangchow, made from young mulberry leaves and served at any time.

Te Kwan Yin
The Iron Goddess of Mercy. This is a rather thin black tea, from Fukien Province. It is grown on steep cliffs and is gathered by monkeys. Te Kwan Yin is usually served in small cups like a fine brandy.

Woo Lung
A black tea from Chinkiang Province, with a good, smoky flavor. It is usually served at public teahouses where people talk for hours over endless cups of this popular tea.

Wun Mo
"Cloud Mist Tea," a green tea from Kiangsi Province, where it is grown in high, mountainous areas and is plucked and gathered by trained monkeys. Wun Mo is usually taken in the afternoon or at tea time.

HOW TO PREPARE CHINESE TEA

The Chinese pay great attention to the preparation of their favorite beverage in order to always obtain the best results.

1. Use a china teapot, never a metal container, as this will reduce the flavor of the tea.

2. Make sure that the water is fresh before bringing it to a strong boil.

3. Preheat the teapot by rinsing it out with some of the boiling water.

4. Use 1 tablespoon tea leaves for a pot that holds approximately 3 cups water. This will make a light tea, which I prefer. Use more tea if you prefer a darker tea.

5. Pour the boiling water over the tea leaves and let them brew in the pot for a few minutes before serving.

Note: I personally prefer a pot of fresh tea, but many Chinese make their tea stronger and then use the same tea leaves with renewed portions of hot water to make more tea. If you prefer this method, do not reuse the same tea leaves for more than 2 hours.

6

CHINESE INGREDIENTS AND WHERE TO BUY THEM

Chinese cuisine is unique for its extraordinary range in flavor and texture, a result of the Chinese chef's use of all edible materials available to him. While creativity is important in preparing standard dishes or in creating new ones, the Chinese cook is aided by a seemingly endless choice of ingredients at his disposal and a truly endless choice of how to combine them. In most instances when the Chinese chef lacks an ingredient— a particular vegetable, sauce, or seasoning—he simply substitutes another, a fact that should encourage Westerners who want to try their hand at Chinese cooking but have no source of Oriental supplies close at hand. When possible, compatible substitutions are suggested in the list of ingredients which make up this chapter.

Because the Chinese believe that eating should promote health, you will find vegetables, nuts, fish, poultry, meat, and seasonings complementing one another in taste, texture, and nutritive value to produce food that is not only delicious and attractive, but that encourages good health as well. Further, the method of cooking is meant to retain as much of the nutritional value of the foods as possible. Whatever you eat will not only delight the senses, but will help maintain good health and longevity.

Chinese foods are very much part of the Yin and Yang concept. Yin foods, feminine and cooling to the system, complement Yang foods, masculine and heating to the system. Too much of either upsets the body's balance and causes one to fall ill.

Vegetables and fruits considered Yin, or cooling, include winter melons and cucumbers, bananas, oranges, papayas, pears, and watermelons. Bird's nest is another Yin food. While Yin foods may act as coolants to the body against "heat" upsets such as acne, sore throats, and heat rash, too many such foods can cause stomach cramps, or in any event are bad when suffering from stomach upsets.

Yang foods include peaches, bitter melons, peppercorns, chili peppers, nuts, meats, and shark's fin. Too many at one time can cause "heat" illnesses such as those mentioned above. Conversely, certain illnesses may call for an emphasis on Yang foods, such as meat, to build up strength. On the whole, the concept of Yin and Yang corresponds to the modern Western concept of good nutrition—a large variety of foods, all eaten in moderation.

In the following list of ingredients, I have suggested substitutions in seasonings as well as in those main ingredients that may not be available on short notice. Certain items, such as bird's nest and shark's fin, do not have a substitute, but you can find them easily in Chinese markets. I am also including a list of reliable Chinese grocery stores at which you can buy the ingredients listed in this chapter, in some cases by mail order.

Because the terminology is sometimes confusing, the ingredients are alphabetized as they appear in the recipes. Bitter melons, which are a vegetable and not a melon in the Western sense, appear under *B* for bitter, and winter melons under *W* for winter. Dried black mushrooms are under *D* for dried, straw mushrooms under *S* for straw, and so on.

ABALONE

(*Bao Yue*) A large sea mollusc, with a flattened, oval, slightly spiral shell. Fresh or canned, abalone should be cooked very lightly, or it becomes tough and rubbery. I should like to recommend the canned variety, which is available in Chinese markets, costs less than the dried variety, and is more convenient to prepare. Once opened, canned abalone will keep in the refrigerator for as long as two weeks if it is covered with water. Sea scallops are a good substitute.

AGAR-AGAR

(*Dai Choi Goo*) A dried, crinkly, translucent gelatin extracted from red seaweed. Sold in bulk or in small packages at any Chinese grocery store.

ANISE PEPPER

(*Fa Chiu*) Also known as Szechuan Pepper, this is a popular spice, with a hotter flavor than ordinary pepper. It is usually used in powdered form, as a dipping, and is available at any Chinese store. It keeps indefinitely if stored in an airtight jar. To make a hot, seasoned salt with Szechuan pepper, heat 3 tablespoons peppercorns in a dry wok, shaking the wok until they start to smoke. Grind in a blender or pound with a mallet until pulverized. Add 3 tablespoons salt and use as desired.

BAMBOO SHOOTS

(*Juk Sun*) Ivory-colored, cone-shaped whole shoots of bamboo, about four inches long, three inches in diameter. They can be bought fresh or canned—whole, diced, sliced, or shredded. The crispness of the bamboo shoot makes it a very popular ingredient in Chinese cooking. To store, rinse and refrigerate in a covered jar filled with water. Bamboo shoots will keep for a long time if the water is changed from time to time. Kohlrabi, or celery shoots, may be substituted for texture, but the taste is very different. Canned bamboo shoots are available at most supermarkets.

BEAN CURD

(*Dow Foo*) Resembles a soft, white cheesecake and measures about three inches square, one-half inch high. It is made by grinding presoftened soybeans with water to form a milk, which is then coagulated to form a soft cake. Because the flavor of soybeans is basically bland, bean curd mixes well with more highly seasoned foods. Vegetarian Buddhists call it "the meat without bones" because of its high protein content. A highly nutritious and inexpensive food, it can be eaten chilled and seasoned, or it can be cooked. To store, cover with water and refrigerate in an open jar. If water is changed daily, bean curd keeps up to two weeks.

BEAN SPROUTS

(*Ngah Choi*) These are shoots germinated from mung beans (small) and from soybeans (bigger and harder). The small variety is the more popular and available of the two. Bean sprouts are crisp and crunchy and are used as a main ingredient in both vegetable and meat dishes. They are generally inexpensive and readily available. They taste best if used the same day and can be combined with almost any seasoning one likes. Since the fresh variety is easily found, I would recommend it over the canned. Bean sprouts store well in the refrigerator for about three days. To prepare, rinse in cold water to cleanse, and pick off or trim the ends. The podlike part is full of nutrients.

BEAN THREADS

(*Fun See*) Also known as cellophane noodles, these threadlike white noodles are made from mung beans. They are stiff and crinkled when dry, but become soft, gelatinous, and transparent when soaked. Cellophane noodles are used in soups and in vegetable dishes.

BÊCHE-DE-MER
(*Hai Sum*) This popular Chinese ingredient is simply a sea slug. Tasteless, it is used more for its jellylike texture when cooked. It is usually braised in a lightly seasoned sauce and takes its flavor from other ingredients in the dish. It is sold dried and wrapped in cellophane, and is available at any Chinese market. It is quite expensive, but in its dried state, keeps indefinitely.

BIRD'S NEST
(*Yeen Woh*) An absolute must at Chinese banquets and formal dinners. It is rich in protein and is extracted from the nests of cliff-dwelling swallows on isolated islands off Southeast Asia. It is a translucent, gelatinous substance, sold in see-through packages. Bird's nest is harvested, dried, and purified before packaging. There are two grades; the cheaper requires more cleaning to remove bird feathers and seeds. Both, however, must be cleaned meticulously and soaked overnight. Bird's nest is one of those prized ingredients the Chinese believe add to a woman's femininity. It is considered an important tonic in convalescence.

BITTER MELON
(*Foo Gwa*) As its name suggests, this is a very bitter vegetable. About the size of a cucumber, sometimes larger, it has a shiny green, bumpy surface, and a pithy interior with bright red seeds. The pith and seeds are always removed before cooking. I usually plunge the sliced bitter melon into boiling water to remove some of the bitter taste. Another method is to slice and soak it in salted water for about an hour before squeezing the water and bitter juices out; it is then rinsed and cooked. I like to quick-fry this vegetable with garlic and black bean sauce. It is available by weight at Chinese groceries. Zucchini makes a satisfactory substitute.

BLACK MOSS
(*Fatt Choy*) Also known as Hair Seaweed, because in its dried form, it looks like a mass of tangled hair. It must be soaked before using, and becomes soft and

gelatinous. Because its name, "Fatt Choy," is part of the Chinese New Year Greeting "Kung Hee Fatt Choy" and suggests prosperity and money, it is always part of the New Year food. Used in vegetable dishes, it takes its flavor from the seasonings used. Black moss is available at Chinese grocery stores and supermarkets in small two-ounce plastic packages, which keep indefinitely in the pantry.

BOK CHOY
See CHINESE WHITE CABBAGE.

BROWN BEAN SAUCE
(*Mein See*) This is a thick, brown sauce made from fermented soybeans, flour, and salt. It can be bought in one-pound cans or jars in Chinese groceries. Because it is so highly flavored,

Mein See is used to season many bland dishes.

CELLOPHANE NOODLES
See BEAN THREADS.

CHEKIANG VINEGAR
The classic vinegar used in Chinese cooking, from Chekiang Province. Almost black in color and with a pungent fragrance, it is used in meat and fish dishes, including shark's fin soup. The best quality is quite thick. My dear friend, the late Madame Sun Yat-sen, kindly presented me with two bottles when I visited her in 1978, because she knew that it was difficult to obtain it in the United States.

CHESTNUTS
(*Lee Chee*) These versatile nuts play an important role in exotic Chinese cookery and, as they are

in Western cuisines, lend themselves to use in sweets as well as in vegetable and meat dishes. You can buy them shelled, halved, and dried, or you can buy them fresh, by the pound. Chinese dried chestnuts keep indefinitely in a jar, if stored in the refrigerator.

CHINESE BACON
(*Yin Yoke*) This widely used ingredient in Chinese cooking is actually smoked pork and comes in a whole pork leg or in chunks, sold by the pound. The reddish-brown meat is tender and juicy. It stores indefinitely. Reasonably good substitutes are cured sausage and lean bacon.

CHINESE BROCCOLI
(*Gai Lan*) A seasonal, bright green vegetable that has the texture of American broccoli, with

a more delicate flavor. Chinese broccoli is inexpensive and is considered good for the digestion. It keeps well refrigerated in a plastic bag and goes well with oyster sauce or with beef. A tasty substitute is American broccoli.

CHINESE CELERY CABBAGE

(*Sieu Choi*) A vegetable that resembles celery, but has loose stalks with large dark green leaves and grows to about one foot in length. The newcomer to Chinese cooking may mistake it for celery, but it cannot be eaten raw. Store in the refrigerator like any other vegetable. American cabbage is a good substitute.

CHINESE CHIVES

(*Gow Choi*) An herb that is almost identical to American chives and is frequently used to flavor beef, pork, and fish dishes. Store the way you would American chives, which provide an exact substitute.

CHINESE DRIED OYSTERS

(*Ho See*) Packed dried and used mainly as a flavoring, they are fishy in taste and aroma. Dried oysters require prolonged soaking, overnight or longer, so that the grit and sand can be easily removed. They are inexpensive and can be bought at any Chinese grocery. Dried oysters will keep indefinitely if stored in airtight containers or in plastic bags.

CHINESE EGG NOODLES

(*Dahm Mein*) Long, thin noodles, about one-eighth of an inch wide, made from flour, eggs, and water. They are sold by the pound, either fresh or dried.

These noodles are used in soups and meat dishes. Cook in boiling hot water, rinse in cold water, and drain. Toss with 1 tablespoon vegetable oil to give them a sheen and to prevent them from sticking together. To store, fresh noodles should always be kept in a plastic bag in the refrigerator, where they will stay fresh for up to two weeks. Egg noodles are available at any Chinese market.

CHINESE EGGPLANT

(*Ai Gwa*) This is a longer and thinner version of the American eggplant, containing fewer seeds. In some Southeast Asian countries there's a green variety as well, used interchangeably with the purple. Inexpensive, they are carried in season by most supermarkets. A good substitute is American eggplant.

CHINESE HAM

(*Foh Toi*) This is a must for Chinese banquet dishes, adding flavor and aroma to them. The darker the color of the meat, the better its flavor. Chinese Ham is a delicacy and cannot be obtained here. The closest substitute is VIRGINIA HAM, discussed later in this chapter.

CHINESE MELON

(*Jik Gwa*) A somewhat tasteless vegetable, about the size of a cucumber, with a rough green skin. It is peeled and seeded before cooking, and is usually stuffed with meat and steamed. It is sometimes used in soups with pork, or on its own stir-fried, or made into a clear soup seasoned with garlic and a little soy sauce. Cooked in either of these ways, it is a popular vegetarian ingredient. Chinese melon is available at all Oriental markets and keeps like other vegetables, in the vegetable compartment of your refrigerator. Zucchini is a reasonable substitute.

CHINESE PARSLEY

(*Yuen Sai*) The same as coriander or cilantro. Chinese parsley is used as a garnish and adds a brisk flavor to soups and meat and poultry dishes. It can be bought at any Chinese or Spanish market and at some supermarkets.

CHINESE PEA PODS

(*Lahn Dow*) Also known as Snow Peas, these are pale green, flat edible pea pods with tiny peas inside. They have a tender, crisp texture and are slightly sweet. Pea pods are usually stir-fried to retain their freshness. The tough strings on the side should be removed before cooking. Available at Chinese markets and some larger supermarkets.

CHINESE SAUSAGE

(*Lap Cheong*) One of the most popular Chinese cooking ingredients is the Chinese sausage. It is made of cured, highly spiced pork and is found hanging in bunches in Chinese markets. This tasty delight is steamed over white rice until the fat is translucent, or it is thin-sliced and stir-fried with other ingredients. It keeps like ham, which is also a reasonable substitute.

CHINESE WATERCRESS

(*Sih Yong Choi*) Similar to the American variety, but with a slightly acid flavor. Used as a garnish, flavoring, and as a main ingredient in soups, it is available in Chinese groceries. A good substitute is American water-cress.

CHINESE WHITE CABBAGE
(*Bok Choi*) This is a very popular ingredient in Chinese cooking because it is easy to obtain and easy to cook. Its leaves are white in color, the tips bordering on pale green. It is crunchy and firm when raw and remains crisp when cooked. Since it does not have any particular taste, Chinese white cabbage absorbs the flavors of the spices and seasonings it is cooked with. Goes well in soups, braised and stir-fried dishes. Usually obtainable at supermarkets and Chinese markets. Keeps up to a week in a plastic bag in the refrigerator. A good substitute is lettuce.

CHINESE WHITE RADISH
(*Loh Bak*) A member of the tur-nip family, this vegetable grows from six to ten inches in length. It has a light tan skin, with a crisp, white flesh and a sharp, piquant taste. It is good raw, eaten in salads, and is also used in soups. The Chinese regard it as a good medicine for a cold. Chinese white radish is available at all Oriental markets. The American white turnip is a substitute.

CLOUD EARS
(*Wun Yee*) A black, gelatinous substance found growing on the bark of trees. It is usually preserved by sun-drying, which turns it gray-brown. To use, cloud ears must be soaked, in the process of which they turn to a dark brown color and expand several times in size. When cooked, they add a crisp, crunchy texture to the dish, tak-ing their flavor from the other ingredients and seasonings. Cloud ears keep well after soaking if immersed in water in a covered jar and refrigerated. While relatively inexpensive in the Orient, they are difficult to come by here and therefore cost more. A close substitute is DRIED BLACK MUSHROOMS.

CORNSTARCH
(*Dow Fun*) This is the standard thickening agent used in Chinese cooking. It is preferred to flour because it gives a translucent sheen to sauces, and is also used in coating batters as it adds crispness to deep-fried foods. It is an inexpensive and effective tenderizer of meats, and I would recommend it over commercial brands of tenderizer as it contains no preservatives. Cornstarch must always be dissolved

in a cold liquid before adding to sauces.

DRIED BEAN CURD SHEETS

(*Dow Fu Pa*) Sold in sheets of various sizes at Chinese markets, the most popular size is a twenty-four-inch circle. These sheets are made from the skin that forms during the process of making bean curds. This vitamin-rich "skin" is sun-dried after being carefully removed from the top of the bean curd. Vegetarian monks use these sheets as a high-protein substitute for meat.

DRIED BLACK MUSHROOMS

(*Dung Goo*) These dried and somewhat gnarled and dull in color mushrooms are extremely popular with Chinese cooks and gourmets. They must be soaked in warm water for fifteen to thirty minutes before cooking. There are three varieties, of which the least expensive, a light, thin mushroom, is also the least tender; the moderately expensive variety is smaller but thicker; and the most expensive variety is light and thick. These last are called "flower mushrooms," and are best for soups as they have the finest flavor. For general cooking, I recommend the second type. Dried black mushrooms keep indefinitely in a cool, dry place. Once soaked, they should be refrigerated in a covered bowl of water. Black mushrooms are available at any Oriental market.

DRIED CUTTLEFISH

(*Yow Yu*) Very much like baby squid, but added to dishes in small quantities because of its very fishy smell. It must be presoaked before cooking and is usually used in soups or is stir-fried, as it does not take long to cook. Available at Chinese markets, it keeps indefinitely in its dried state in plastic bags. It may be too strong, however, for Western tastes.

DRIED JELLYFISH

(*Hai Jit Pa*) A seafood used widely in Chinese cooking, sold in a dehydrated form. Jellyfish look coarse and have a dull brown color when dry, but after soaking overnight take on a crisp, gelatinous texture, and turn a paler shade of brown. Almost tasteless, they are used in cold dishes where they borrow the flavors of the other ingredients and seasonings. They are expensive to buy, but even so it is better to buy the best quality. Some Chinese markets stock a preshredded variety that makes it easier to handle. DRIED JELLYFISH keep indefinitely in the pantry.

DRIED RED DATES
(*Hung Jo*) Inexpensive, light, sweet flavored, and scented fruits that are used in desserts. They are sometimes mashed into a paste and can be purchased in this form. Available at Chinese markets, they must be soaked before using, but keep indefinitely in their dry state in an airtight jar.

DRIED SCALLOPS
(*Gong Yu Chee*) Similar to the American variety, but shrunken. They are amber colored and must be soaked before using. When cooked, they are tough and chewy, with a fishy, slightly sweet flavor. Dried scallops are used in combination with other ingredients. Store in a covered glass jar. DRIED SHRIMP are a reasonable substitute. Dried scallops can be bought at Chinese markets.

DRIED SEAWEED
(*Gee Choi*) Also known as the "paper" vegetable, because of its thin crinkliness in the dried state. When cooked, it becomes soft and jellylike. Seaweed is excellent in soups and is available at all Oriental groceries.

DRIED SHRIMP
(*Har Mai*) Tiny dried shrimp, amber colored, with a sharp, salty taste. They are used as a flavoring ingredient, especially in bland vegetable dishes or sometimes with congee. They have a strong, fishy aroma and must be soaked before using. They are sold by weight at all Oriental stores and keep for a long time in a covered glass jar.

DRIED TANGERINE PEEL
(*Chin Pei*) The dried rind of the tangerine, crinkled and dull in appearance, and with a fragrant orange-peel aroma. Tart and sweet at the same time, it is slightly spicy as well. It is used as an unusual flavoring for meat dishes, and also as a stuffing and a garnish. It can be bought at any Chinese market and keeps indefinitely.

EGG ROLL SKINS
(*Chuen Guen Pei*) Ready-made wrappers for egg rolls that come in six-inch squares of one-eighth-inch thickness. They

have a fresh white color, a thin, doughy feel, and are wonderfully crisp when fried. They can be bought at Chinese markets fresh, by the pound, and can be refrigerated three to four days or well wrapped and stored in the freezer where they will keep for several months.

FERMENTED BEAN CAKE

(*Fu Yu*) This is truly the "cheese" of Chinese cuisine. It is a soft, moist, tender substance, with a smooth surface, and comes in one-half- to one-inch cubes packed tightly in glass jars. Found at most Chinese groceries. Because of its strong, cheesy taste and pungent aroma, fermented bean curd is used as a spicy flavoring. It can be stored unopened indefinitely and will keep as long when opened, if refrigerated.

FIVE-SPICE POWDER

(*Ng Heung Fun*) A powdered blend of star anise, fennel, cinnamon, clove, and ANISE PEPPER, used sparingly as a flavoring agent for meat and poultry. It is sold by weight or in little boxes at Chinese groceries. You can make your own substitute by combining the different spices, or you can use allspice instead.

FRESH NOODLES

(*Lo Mein*) A whitish, doughy Chinese noodle made of rice flour and a little egg. They are sold in eight-ounce packages, wound closely together. These noodles have no flavor of their own, absorbing the taste of the other ingredients and seasonings. They keep several days when refrigerated and are available at Chinese groceries.

FUN SEE

See BEAN THREADS.

GARLIC

(*Seun Tao*) This is popular in Chinese cooking and is used to flavor stir-fried vegetable and meat dishes. It is also mashed and used with brown beans as a seasoning and sometimes is used as a main flavoring for highly spiced Szechuan or Hunan cooking.

GINGERROOT

(*Sang Geong*) A gnarled, beige-colored root, about three inches long, with a yellow-beige flesh. It is frequently used as a basic flavoring agent and adds a delicate pungency to food. Its strong aroma, for instance, masks the strong odor of seafood. Ginger is used as a main ingredient in several stir-fried dishes, usually with beef or pork. It is usually used peeled and cut into one-half-inch slices. To store, keep in the refrigerator for up to a month. Gingerroot can be obtained from Chinese markets and some supermarkets.

GLUTINOUS RICE
(*Noh Mai*) A good-tasting rice that is about the size of long-grain rice, but somewhat more rounded in shape. It becomes soft and sticky when cooked. Glutinous rice is used in ceremonial dishes and in desserts, such as Eight Precious Rice Pudding. It also makes a good stuffing base for roast turkey and duck. You can buy this rice by weight and it is available in Chinese markets.

GLUTINOUS RICE FLOUR
(*Noh Mai Fun*) A flour ground from glutinous rice and used in sweet dishes or desserts. It is sold by weight and is available at Chinese groceries. Store as you would regular flour, in a covered container.

GOLDEN NEEDLES
(*Gum Jum*) Also known as Dried Lily Flowers, these are the dried stems of the Chinese tiger lily. They are softened in water before cooking, first removing a hard, stemlike strand from the main length. These two- to three-inch stems are cooked as vegetables, but have the delicate flavor of beef broth. They keep indefinitely in their dried state if stored in a cool place. Golden needles are widely used in vegetarian cooking and go well with stir-fried vegetables. They can be bought at Chinese groceries.

HOISIN SAUCE
(*Hoi Sin Jeung*) A thick, brownish-red sauce made up of soybean flour, red beans, ginger, garlic, spices, salt, sugar, and a little chili. It has a tangy-sweet taste and is a flavoring ingredient for all kinds of meat, poultry, and seafood. It is very versatile, blending well with other sauces and perking up the flavor of any bland foods. Hoisin sauce is sold in one-pound cans or jars, or in larger amounts. It keeps indefinitely if stored in a covered glass jar in the refrigerator. It can be bought at any Chinese grocery. Anyone who cooks Chinese style with regularity should always have some on hand. Good substitutes are PLUM SAUCE, or catsup and soy sauce mixed with a little sugar.

HOT SAUCE

(*Lok Yow*) A ready-made sauce that is used as a seasoning and is made of ground chili and spices. It is inexpensively purchased in five- to six-ounce jars at any Chinese market as well as at some supermarkets. Refrigerated, it keeps indefinitely.

KUMQUATS

(*Kumquat*) Popular small, oval fruits, which are a dark tangerine in color with a pungent, sweet aroma. The sweet exterior surrounds the tart inner flesh. Kumquats can be purchased fresh, preserved, or crystallized. Preserved in syrup, they are available in six-ounce jars or by the gallon and keep indefinitely in the refrigerator. Crystallized kumquats are sold by the pound, or in smaller quantities, in pre-

sealed plastic packets at Chinese markets.

LICHEES

(*Lychee*) A small oval fruit with a rough skin, juicy white pulp, and a large black pit. It is a seasonal fruit that can be purchased fresh in June and early July at Chinese markets. They are also canned in syrup and there are some markets which sell a thick lichee syrup that is mixed with water for a cool, refreshing drink. Served at formal Chinese dinners, usually with almond-flavored jelly, in place of longans.

LILY FLOWERS

(*Gum Tsum*) Also known as Tiger Lily Flowers, this unusual ingredient is the dried bud of the tiger lily. It is golden brown in color and has to be softened in water before cooking. It lends a slightly sweet and distinctive taste to vegetable and poultry dishes. Lily flowers can be bought at Chinese groceries and keep for an indefinite period of time in their dried state.

LONGANS

(*Loong Ngan*) Sometimes known as Dragon's Eyes, they are another popular Chinese fruit. They are round, from one-half to one inch in size, and have a slightly tough, smooth skin. The flesh is translucent and tender and is usually sweet and juicy. The pit is hard, round, and dark. They are delicious fresh, but as such can only be obtained seasonally, when they are sold by the pound. They are also available dried and canned, packed in syrup. An approximate substitute for longans in their dried form is raisins. Canned or fresh lichees make the best alternative. Fresh longans are available at Chinese groceries during late July and August.

LONG GREEN BEANS
(*Dow Gok*) These are the equivalent of runner beans; grow from sixteen to thirty-two inches; and have a dull, smooth, green surface. They are chopped into bite-size segments and should be cooked lightly, to retain their crispness. They can be flavored in many ways and go well with most meat dishes. Store in the vegetable tray of the refrigerator. Long green beans can be inexpensively bought at any Chinese market.

LOQUATS
(*Pei Pa*) A round orange fruit, about one to two inches in diameter. Their juicy, tender, and delicate-tasting flesh makes them another popular Chinese dessert. They are usually canned, packed in syrup, and in this form keep several days in a refrigerator after opening. When dried, they are eaten like prunes. You can buy loquats at any Chinese market at a reasonable price. Substitutes are LICHEES and LONGANS.

LOTUS ROOTS
(*Leen Ngow*) Long tubular roots attached to each other like a string of sausages. Lotus roots have a thin, beige skin, like a potato, and a white interior with holes like Swiss cheese. They are used chiefly in soups and vegetable dishes, but their sweet aroma and delicate taste lend themselves to desserts. One particularly delicious dessert is made by stuffing the peeled roots with a sweet paste and steaming and slicing them. They are also candied as sweetmeats, and as such are enjoyed by Chinese children who nibble on them as a treat. Lotus roots can be purchased in many forms at Chinese markets: fresh, by the whole root and weight; dried and sliced; sliced, canned, and packed in water; powdered (stem only); sugared, in cellophane or plastic packets. It is expensive, but makes an unusual ingredient, keeps well in its various forms, and can be bought in small quantities.

MELON SEEDS
(*Gwa Chee*) These are dried watermelon seeds and are eaten like

nuts. Red or black in color, the husk is removed before eating. Melon seeds are slightly sweet and make a delicious, low-calorie snack. They can be purchased inexpensively at any Chinese market and keep for an indefinite period of time.

OYSTER SAUCE
(*Ho Yao*) A popular flavoring sauce, used with a large number of dishes. It is thick and brown, with a meaty yet delicate aroma and flavor. Oyster sauce also enhances the appearance of the dishes it is cooked with, adding a sheen to the food. The best kind is imported from Macao and makes a good dipping and frying sauce. Oyster sauce is salty, however, so reduce the amount of salt in the dish when using it. Available in bottles or cans, from any Chinese market,

it should be refrigerated after opening. A good substitute is a mixture of juice from canned oysters, dark soy sauce, and a little catsup.

PLUM SAUCE
(*Suhn Mui Jeung*) A thick reddish-brown sauce with a sweet and pungent flavor, made from plums, apricots, chilis, vinegar, and sugar. Widely used as a dip for roast duck, plum sauce is sold bottled or canned and is available at all Chinese markets. Canned plum sauce should be transferred to a jar before storing in a refrigerator.

RED BEAN PASTE
(*Hung Dow Sah*) A thick, sweet paste made from red soybeans and used in desserts. It is rather tasty, similar to dates. Available in cans in Chinese groceries, it

will keep for months after opening, if stored in a covered jar in the refrigerator.

RED BEANS
(*Hung Dow*) Tiny smooth red beans used in soups and in pastes for sweet dishes and desserts. It is sold by weight in Oriental markets.

RICE STICKS
(*Mai Fun*) These are packaged thin white noodles, similar in appearance before cooking to CELLOPHANE NOODLES, but with a different texture. They have little flavor of their own, and, like other noodles, take on the flavor of other ingredients in the dish. They are added to other ingredients after cooking, either by deep-frying to a crisp puffiness, or by boiling. Rice sticks are available at all Chinese markets

and at some supermarkets in one-pound packages.

SALTED BLACK BEANS
(*Dow See*) These are small fermented black beans that have a sharp, salty taste. They must be washed before using and are available in plastic bags and cans in Chinese markets. They are often mashed with garlic and used as a seasoning. A prepared BROWN BEAN SAUCE may be substituted. Salted black beans keep well after opening if stored covered in the refrigerator.

SALTED DUCK EGGS
(*Hahm Dan*) These are cured in black clay and brine for thirty days or more and are bought individually. The clay is washed away and the egg boiled and cut into wedges before eating. Salted duck eggs are used as a main dish and go well with lightly seasoned vegetables, white rice, or congee. They are sometimes steamed whole with meat. Available at Chinese groceries, salted eggs will keep a long time if the clay packing is retained. However, if they have already been cooked and shelled, they will keep for about two weeks in the refrigerator. You can make your own substitute by soaking hen's eggs in brine for three to four weeks.

SALT FISH
(*Hahn Yu*) Very popular with the Chinese, there are many varieties of salted fish, some fleshy, some small and bony. A relatively inexpensive form of protein that keeps for an indefinite period, their strong fishy flavor is often unpalatable to Westerners. The Chinese, however, use salted fish as a main ingredient, blended with meat or eaten with bland foods like congee. Salted fish is available at all Chinese markets.

SCALLIONS
(*Chin Chong*) We use the white bulb and about six inches of the green stem in our cooking. Scallions are often used with gingerroot as a seasoning for fish and meat. When used in this manner, they are usually tied into a knot with their own stem, then discarded before serving. Often they are chopped and used as a garnish or a table seasoning, or cut into little brooms and served with duck. They add a little extra to the overall flavor of the food they are used with. They are available at all supermarkets. You will probably know them as green onions.

SESAME OIL

(*Gee Mah Yao*) An amber-colored oil from ROASTED SESAME SEEDS, with a delightful and delicate flavor. Sesame oil is used in small quantities to lift the flavor of the food. Try a few drops with salad or any bland dish. For cooked food, sesame oil should be added at the very last minute, just before the food is removed from the wok or skillet, as prolonged cooking ruins the delicate flavor and scent.

SESAME SEEDS

(*Gee Mah*) These tiny, flat seeds may be black or white, depending upon the variety. In China black sesame seeds are said to stimulate the growth of hair. Sesame seeds have a delicate flavor and are used in desserts. An imported variety is available in many supermarkets.

SHARK'S FIN

(*Yu Chee*) The translucent, threadlike, dried cartilage from a shark's fin is expensive and considered a delicacy. Gelatinous and bland when cooked, it is always used with red-cooked meat and poultry in the form of a thick, flavored soup, along with thin-sliced dried black mushrooms and sometimes carrots. Shark's fin is always served at Chinese weddings (it is believed to promote virility) and at formal dinners. It can be bought dried or in cans, the canned variety having been partly prepared by having the skin and sand removed. The dried variety keeps for years in the pantry and is sometimes hard to find, but the canned variety is almost always available in Chinese markets.

SHRIMP PASTE

(*Hahm Har*) A purply-white, thick paste made from shrimp and shellfish, with a pungent and fishy aroma and taste. It is used sparingly as a flavoring agent, as it is very salty. Probably a little strong for Western tastes, it can be bought in small jars, up to eight ounces. It will keep indefinitely in the refrigerator.

SILVER EARS

(*Ngan Yee*) Also known as White Fungus. It is a translucent version of CLOUD EARS, sometimes referred to as Albino. Silver ears are a somewhat expensive delicacy and are used in hot and cold desserts. They are transparent and jellylike when cooked and easily digestible. Silver ears are obtainable at Chinese groceries and keep indefinitely in the pantry in their dried form.

SNOW PEAS
See CHINESE PEA PODS.

SOY SAUCE
(*See Yao*) A salty brown liquid made from fermented soybeans, wheat flour, salt, yeast, and water. The imported Chinese and Japanese sauces are good buys. Soy sauce varies in thickness and shade from dark to light, with the lighter sauce containing more salt. Soy sauce is used as a main flavoring ingredient for many Chinese dishes and you will not find a Chinese kitchen without a bottle each of dark and light sauce. Soy sauce is available at all markets.

STAR ANISE
(*Bat Gok*) A licorice-flavored spice, with a burnt sienna color,

it looks like an eight-pointed star, of up to about one-and-a-half inches in width. I prefer to use the powdered form as I can control the amount used more accurately. One of the spices in FIVE-SPICE POWDER, star anise can be bought at any Chinese grocery or in spice shops. It keeps indefinitely stored in an airtight container.

STRAW MUSHROOMS
(*Chao Goo*) These are available canned from mainland China. In China, straw mushrooms are considered a delicacy. They are smooth and tender and have a delicate flavor. They come packed in water, in eight-ounce cans, and are available at Chinese groceries.

SZECHUAN CABBAGE TIPS
These are an interesting product

of the Szechuan school of cooking. Regular Chinese cabbage tips are preserved in brine and highly seasoned with spices and chili. Szechuan cabbage tips are usually available in cans, which can be obtained at any Chinese grocery. Makes an exciting addition to stir-fried meat, poultry, and seafood dishes, or as a zesty accompaniment on its own with rice and blander foods.

THOUSAND-YEAR-OLD EGGS
(*Pay Dahn*) These are regular hens' eggs which are covered with a paste made of ashes, lime, and salt for about 100 days. This slow-baking process turns the white of the egg into a translucent brownish-black, and the yolk to a gray, with a mild, cheeselike flavor. To use, wash the eggs thoroughly, shell, and

slice. They are featured as part of the hors d'oeuvres or cold dish course at a formal Chinese dinner, or eaten as a flavoring with congee. Thousand- (or hundred) year-old eggs can be purchased individually from Chinese markets. Unshelled and in their original packing, they will keep indefinitely. If shelled, they will keep in the refrigerator several weeks.

TI LEAVES
(*Ho Yet*) The dried leaves of the ti plant, which are used to wrap dumplings. These leaves, up to 1 foot in length, are used in place of lotus leaves, which are not easily obtainable outside Asia. Ti leaves have a slight scented aroma and this adds a scented lift to the food they are wrapped around. Obtainable at Chinese groceries in one-pound bundles,

ti leaves keep indefinitely in dried form in the pantry.

TIGER LILY FLOWERS
See LILY FLOWERS.

VIRGINIA HAM
(*Foh Toi*) This ham is the closest possible substitute for Chinese ham. A cured, smoked ham, it can be bought by the slice in Chinese markets, gourmet shops, and supermarkets. It will keep several weeks if stored in the refrigerator wrapped in foil. Substitutes are Italian prosciutto or Westphalian ham.

WATER CHESTNUTS
(*Mah Tai*) Dark brown bulbs, packed in mud to keep them from drying out. To use, wash off the mud, peel, and cut as you wish. Water chestnuts have a crisp texture and are delicate, sweet, and juicy to the taste.

They are usually eaten raw, and are used sliced in vegetable and poultry dishes. Also available in cans, these are not as tasty as the fresh variety. To store canned water chestnuts, pour the liquid out, rinse the chestnuts in clear water, and refrigerate them packed in water in a covered jar. They are available both fresh and canned in Oriental markets.

WHEAT STARCH
(*Yuen Fun*) Similar to cornstarch, but is the starchy flour extract of wheat, wheat starch is used in some Chinese doughs and gravied dishes. Obtainable in one-pound packets at Chinese groceries, it keeps like cornstarch or flour.

WINTER MELON
(*Dung Gwa*) This vegetable, used for soup, is the size of a water-

melon and has the same green color, overlaid with a frosty white. The white flesh becomes translucent when cooked. To use, peel, remove pith and seeds, and slice or cut into chunks. A more elaborate presentation, used at formal Chinese dinners and banquets, is to cut off the top and scoop out the flesh for cooking. The soup is cooked and served in the melon shell (see WINTER MELON SOUP, page 25). Winter melon may be bought whole or by slice at all Chinese markets. Cut in sections, it will keep in the refrigerator for about a week; whole, it will keep for several months in a cool, dark place.

WON TON SKINS
(*Won Ton Pae*) A dough made from flour, water, and eggs, it is sold in three-inch squares at Chinese markets. These are used for won tons and spring rolls. Store in a clean, wet towel in the refrigerator, where they will remain fresh and moist for up to five days.

YEE FU NOODLES
(*Yee Fu Mein*) A convenience noodle, packaged in portions of one or two servings and flavored with a variety of seasonings—chicken, beef, shrimp, mushroom, or pork. They are wonderful as a light lunch and go well with other ingredients. Flavored noodles are available at any Chinese market and at some supermarkets.

A SHOPPING GUIDE TO CHINESE INGREDIENTS

Following is a list of reliable Chinese groceries and markets at which Chinese ingredients are available. Those places with mail order departments are marked with an asterisk (*). The prices are generally constant with these shops and the range of goods is competitive.

California

China Native Products, Inc.
970 North Broadway
Los Angeles, CA 90012

Gim Fat Co., Inc.
953 Grant Avenue
San Francisco, CA 94018

Kwong Dack Wo Co.
702 North Spring Street
Los Angeles, CA 90012

*Kwong On Lung Co.
922 South San Pedro Street
Los Angeles, CA 90015

Kwong On Teong
720 Webster Street
Oakland, CA 94607

Mandarin Trading Co.
102 Mandarin Plaza
970 North Broadway
Los Angeles, CA 90012

Moon John
830 Grant Avenue
San Francisco, CA 94108

*Mow Lee Sing Kee Co.
730 Grant Avenue
San Francisco CA 94108

*Mow Lee Shing Kee Co.
774 Commercial Street
San Francisco, CA 94111

Wing Chong Co.
367 Eighth Street
Oakland, CA 94607

*Wing Chong Lung Co.
922 South San Pedro Street
Los Angeles, CA 90015

Wing Sing Chong Co.
1076 Stockton Street
San Francisco, CA 94108

Yee Sing Chong Co.
960 North Hill Street
Los Angeles, CA 90012

Yick Chong Co.
423 "J" Street
Sacramento, CA 95831

District of Columbia

Mee Wah Lung Co.
608 H Street N.W.
Washington, DC 20001

New China Supply Co.
709 H Street N.W.
Washington, DC 20001

Tuck Cheong & Co.
716 H Street
Washington, DC 20001

Illinois

China Farms
733 West Randolph Street
Chicago, Illinois

*Kam Shing Co.
2246 South Wentworth Street
Chicago, IL 60616

Massachusetts

Chung Lung
18 Hudson Street
Boston, MA 02143

Sun See Co.
36 Harrison Avenue
Boston, MA 02111

Sun Sun
34 Oxford Street
Boston, MA 02138

T. H. Lung
9 Hudson Street
Boston, MA 02143

Wing Wing
79 Harrison Avenue
Boston, MA 02111

New York

Kam Kuo Food Corp.
7–9 Mott Street
New York, NY 10013

*Mon Fong Wo Co.
36 Pell Street
New York, NY 10013

*Oriental Food Shop
1032 Amsterdam Avenue
New York, NY 10027

Wing Woh Lung
50 Mott Street
New York, NY 10013

Wo Fat Co.
16 Bowery
New York, NY 10013

Oregon

Fong Chong Co.
301 N.W. Fourth Avenue
Portland, OR 97209

Pennsylvania

*Wing On Grocery Store
1005 Race Street
Philadelphia, PA 19107

Texas

*Oriental Import-Export Co.
2009 Polk Street
Houston, TX 77003

Washington

Wah Young Co.
416 Eighth Avenue South East
Seattle, WA 98371

7

GLOSSARY
OF
TERMS

Chinese cuisine has infinite possibilities for innovation and creation, but you must be familiar with the methods, ingredients, and seasonings of the cuisine. This can come only with practice. I am sure that a brief description of some of the terms used in Chinese cooking will aid you in this effort.

CHOP
In Chinese cooking, this means a straight cut of the vegetable, to about the size of a pea. It is usually done with a large, sharp knife, or cleaver.

COATING
In Chinese cooking, coating usually refers to the cornstarch that is mixed in with a sauce in which meat or poultry has been marinated. The cornstarch, which is added a few minutes before cooking, serves as an effective tenderizer, especially for quick-cooking. It also helps to retain the flavor of the meat and prevents the marinade from sticking to the wok or skillet. Batter coatings are usually used for deep-fried seafood and fruit fritters. Cornstarch is also used to coat items for DEEP-FRYING.

COLOR
Color is important to the overall enjoyment of Chinese cuisine. It does not matter what you put into your dish, if the color is not right, it will not look appetizing and may even detract from your enjoyment. STIR-FRYING is a cooking method by which color is retained. Vegetables cooked in this fashion keep their delicious, bright green color if the lid is not removed during the first few minutes of cooking. This fast cooking, facilitated by cutting the vegetables, allows them to retain their color.

CUBE
A method of cutting meat or vegetables, to about one inch square. This is good for vegetables like carrots, zucchini, and cucumbers, and meats like pork.

DEEP-FRYING
As in Western cooking, the correct heat and timing is important in deep-frying. Test for correct temperature by putting a small piece of bread into the hot oil. If it rises to the surface immediately, the oil is ready for use. Do not crowd the pan, so that each portion may be evenly cooked. Deep-frying is used for coated meat and poultry dishes, desserts such as Deep-Fried Milk, and appetizers.

DIAGONAL-SLICE

This is a method of cutting commonly used in Chinese cooking and allows the most exposure to each slice of vegetable. The food is cut at a forty-five-degree angle and a quarter turn is made after each slice. This technique is used for cutting such items as green onions, celery, broccoli, and bok choy into one-and-one-half inch lengths.

DICE

This is another common cutting method in Chinese cooking. The diced product is much smaller than the cube. It is produced by cutting into strips lengthwise and then cutting across these to form little cubes of about one-half inch to three-eighths inch in size.

FINE-SLICE

See THIN-SLICE.

FLAVOR

In Chinese cooking, flavor means the overall taste and appearance of the dish. To obtain a good flavor, the cutting and cooking methods, the spices and seasonings, and the combination of ingredients, must all blend and complement one another.

MINCE

Minced meat or vegetables in Chinese cooking is the same as in any other cuisine and is obtained by finely chopping or putting the ingredient through a grinder. Minced ingredients are used as stuffings and fillings for poultry, won tons, spring rolls, dumplings, and pastries.

QUICK-FRYING

See STIR-FRYING.

RED-COOKING

Called *Haung Siu* in Chinese, this is a method of slowly cooking tough cuts of meat with dark soy sauce. The soy sauce gives the otherwise dull meat flavor, as well as a deep brownish-red color. Red-cooking is unpopular because it is so time consuming.

SHRED

Shredding in Chinese cooking is done by thin-slicing, then cutting into thin strips measuring one inch to one and one-half inches long, one-fourth inch to one-eighth inch wide. Some ingredients, such as chicken, can be pulled apart. Vegetables used in fillings, as garnishes, and for fancy cooking are shredded. Meat is sometimes cut in the same way for intricate dishes.

SQUARE

A method of cutting meat, poultry, and vegetables into chunks of about one and one-half inches on all sides.

STEAMING

This is known as *Jing* in Chinese. The food is placed on the actual serving dishes in a larger container, like a steamer or wok, raised above the water level, so that the water never touches the food. A lid is placed over the wok or steamer, and the steam is allowed to circulate freely all around the food. Steaming is a popular method of cooking as it requires very little attention and delicately enhances flavor. Fish seasoned lightly with salt and ginger is particularly good when steamed.

STEWING

Like Western cooking, stewing is used for meats, particularly the tougher cuts. In Chinese cooking, this term takes us a step further in that soups are prepared in this way, as well as rice.

STIR-FRYING

This term is equivalent to the French cooking term, *sauté*. Stir-frying is really quick-frying or sautéing. The term itself can be misleading, for if you stir and fry meat while it is cooking, it will become watery and tough. What you are actually doing is quick-frying. This is one of the main methods of Chinese cooking and is really an excellent way to keep vegetables crisp yet cooked, meat well coated and colored, yet tender. Stir-frying or quick-frying is, of course, possible only because the ingredients have been cut into bite-size or smaller pieces.

THIN-SLICE

Also means fine-slice, which is a popular method of preparing vegetables for cooking. The slices are still bite-size, about one and one-half inches in length, one inch in width, and one-half inch to one-sixteenth inch thick.

8

CALORIE COUNTS FOR CHINESE INGREDIENTS

In today's health-conscious world, I suppose it wouldn't really be possible to go on any kind of diet without a calorie chart. Chinese food, however, has very few calories to worry about unless, of course, the dishes are deep-fried, or for some reason or another contain more fat than usual. For those of you who do count calories, I am including a calorie chart for Chinese ingredients. I hope it helps you to adjust my Long Life Diet dishes accordingly.

Cereals and Grain Products

		Calories
Flour (all-purpose)	1 cup	499
Rice	1 cup	180
Rice (glutinous)	1 cup	402
Rice noodles (Chinese egg noodles)	1 cup	200
Vermicelli	1 cup	200

Starchy Roots and Stems

Lotus roots	4 ounces	59
Sweet potatoes (red)	4 ounces	128
Water chestnuts	4 ounces	90

Legumes, Seeds, and Nuts

Almonds (dried, shelled, whole)	4 ounces	424
Almonds (roasted in oil, salted)	4 ounces	492
Cashews (roasted in oil)	4 ounces	392

		Calories
Chestnuts (shelled)	4 ounces	220
Lotus seeds	4 ounces	351
Peanuts (shelled, with skins)	4 ounces	664
Pecans (shelled, halved)	4 ounces	371
Red beans	4 ounces	384
Sesame seeds (white)	4 ounces	492
Soybeans	4 ounces	180
Soybean curd (cake)	4 ounces	80
Soybean sauce	4 ounces	202

Oils and Fats

Vegetable oil	1 cup	962

Dairy Products

Cream cheese	4 ounces	424
Egg (white)	4 ounces	30
Egg (yolk)	4 ounces	240

		Calories
Thousand-year-old egg	4 ounces	203

Meat and Poultry Products

Bacon	4 ounces	400
Beef (lean)	4 ounces	277
Beef (with fat)	4 ounces	300
Chicken	4 ounces	132
Chicken liver	4 ounces	150
Chinese sausage	4 ounces	504
Duck (roasted)	4 ounces	208
Ham (boiled)	4 ounces	350
Ham (Virginia)	4 ounces	270
Pork (fat)	4 ounces	935
Pork (lean)	4 ounces	394
Pork (medium)	4 ounces	624
Pork kidney	4 ounces	130

		Calories
Pork spareribs	8 ounces	250
Squab	4 ounces	150
Turkey	4 ounces	250

Seafood and Marine Products

Abalone (canned)	4 ounces	91
Abalone (dried)	4 ounces	351
Abalone (raw)	4 ounces	115
Crab meat	4 ounces	106
Fillet of sole	4 ounces	125
Lobster (canned)	4 ounces	108
Lobster (fresh)	4 ounces	108
Red snapper (meat only)	4 ounces	105
Sea bass (meat only)	4 ounces	110
Shark's fin	4 ounces	428
Shrimp (dried)	4 ounces	224

		Calories
Shrimp (fresh)	4 ounces	103
Squid (dried)	4 ounces	305
Squid (fresh)	4 ounces	93

Vegetables

American broccoli	4 ounces	30
Asparagus (fresh)	4 ounces	20
Asparagus (yellow, canned)	4 ounces	22
Bamboo shoots	4 ounces	20
Bean sprouts	4 ounces	17
Bitter melon (Balsam pear)	4 ounces	15
Brussels sprouts	4 ounces	60
Button mushrooms	4 ounces	20
Cabbage	4 ounces	19
Cauliflower	4 ounces	20

		Calories
Celery	4 ounces	108
Chinese broccoli	4 ounces	33
Chinese greens (Pe-Tsai)	4 ounces	17
Cloud ear fungus	4 ounces	128
Cream-style sweet corn (canned)	4 ounces	90
Cucumber (with skin)	4 ounces	20
Eggplant	4 ounces	25
Ginger	4 ounces	42
Green onion	4 ounces	31
Green peas (fresh or frozen)	4 ounces	40
Green pepper	4 ounces	25
Lettuce	4 ounces	16
Mushrooms (dried black)	4 ounces	146
Mustard pickles	4 ounces	32
Parsley (chopped)	1 ounce	2

		Calories
Pea pods	4 ounces	32
Red cabbage	4 ounces	22
Red pepper	4 ounces	30
Seaweed (agar-agar)	4 ounces	211
Snow peas (Chinese pea pods)	4 ounces	36
Spinach	4 ounces	20
Tomato	4 ounces	25
Turnips	4 ounces	30
Watercress	4 ounces	22
White onion	4 ounces	50
Winter melon	4 ounces	8

Fruits

Apple	4 ounces	80
Banana	4 ounces	100

		Calories
Candied kumquats	4 ounces	74
Candied orange peel	4 ounces	360
Cherries	4 ounces	72
Coconut (dried)	4 ounces	360
Coconut (fresh)	4 ounces	408
Dates (whole)	4 ounces	250
Lichee (dried)	4 ounces	315
Lichee (fresh)	4 ounces	73
Pineapple (canned in water)	4 ounces	50
Raisins (seedless)	4 ounces	210

Miscellaneous

Brown sugar	4 ounces	270
Catsup	1 tablespoon	25
″	4 ounces	106
Champagne	1 champagne glass	105

		Calories
Chicken broth	1 cup	100
Cornstarch	1 ounce	30
Honey	1 tablespoon	62
Lemon juice	1 tablespoon	4
Salt	—	0
Sherry	1 sherry glass	38
Sugar	1 teaspoon	16
Vinegar	4 ounces	12
Wine (red)	1 claret glass	95

INDEX

[Items set in italics denote non-recipes. Recipes are in roman type.]

Soups (*Cont.*):
   lotus root, dragon seed and lean pork, 30
   mushroom spinach, 28
   pheasant chicken giblets and fuzzy melon, 20
   pig's feet and peanut, 21
   salt fish bean curd, 24
   scalded fish and Chinese parsley, 36
   seaweed bean curd, 40
   shark's fin, 23
   soybean sprouts and bean curd, 38
   watercress, 27
   winter melon, 25
Soy sauce, 234
   eggs, 17
Soybean sprouts and bean curd soup, 38
Spareribs, barbecued, 6
Spicy shrimp, 108
Spinach and bamboo shoots, 128
Spinach soup, mushrooms and, 28
Spring rolls:
   chicken, 12
   vegetarian, 11
Squab:
   with ginseng, 178
   minced, with string of jade, 105
   roast, 104
Squid in garlic and black bean sauce, 123
Star anise, 234
Steamed beef cake, 50

Steamed beef with Szechuan cabbage tip, 51
String beans and carrots with leek, 133
String of jade with minced squab, 105
Stuffed eight precious duck with pearls, 97–98
Stuffing, chestnut and red bean, 208
Sweet soup of silver ears and quail eggs, 188
Sweet and sour cabbage salad, 143
Sweet and sour chicken, 88
Sweet and sour pork, 59
Sweet and sour sauce, 171
Sweet and sour whole fish, 121
Szechuan cabbage tip, steamed beef with, 51

Tang kuei, brewed, and chicken, 181
Tangerine peel, dried, 226
Tapioca pudding, mango, 161
Teas, 211–215
   how to prepare, 215
   list of popular Chinese, 213–214
Ti leaves, 235
Tiem joong, 205
Tiger lily flowers, 229
Toast, shrimp, 15
Tomato:
   beef, 52
   cherry, 140
   with eggs and ham, 157

   sauce, Wu's, 173
   soup, cabbage and, 29
Turnips, white, 196

Vegetables, 125–144
   with chicken and mushrooms, 76
Vegetarian spring rolls, 11
Vegetarian's delight, 129
Vermicelli, chicken, 86
Vinegar on pig's feet and ginger, 182

Walnut:
   chicken, 75
   sweet, broth, 166
Water chestnuts, 235
Watercress, 223–224
   with bamboo shoots, 139
   with beef, 114
   soup, 27
Wheat starch, 235
Wine sauce on fillet of fish, 118
Winter melon soup, 25
Won ton skins, 236
Wu's beef with watercress, 44
Wu's garden rumaki, 5
Wu's mustard, 168
Wu's tomato sauce, 173

Yellow croaker with pine nuts, 119–120

Zucchini with mushrooms, 136